Deviant Usage and Confusing Words

Deviant Usage and Confusing Words

Gordon S. K. Adika
Language Centre, University of Ghana
Legon, Ghana

LAXMI PUBLICATIONS (P) LTD
BANGALORE • CHENNAI • COCHIN • GUWAHATI • HYDERABAD
JALANDHAR • KOLKATA • LUCKNOW • MUMBAI • RANCHI • NEW DELHI
INDIA • USA • GHANA • KENYA

DEVIANT USAGE AND CONFUSING WORDS

Printed and bound in India
New Edition
EDU-0798-125-DEVIANT USAGE CONF WORD-ADI
ISBN 978-93-5138-097-9

PUBLISHED IN INDIA BY

Laxmi Publications (P) Ltd.
113, GOLDEN HOUSE, DARYAGANJ,
NEW DELHI - 110002, INDIA
Telephone : 91-11-4353 2500, 4353 2501
Fax : 91-11-2325 2572, 4353 2528
www.laxmipublications.com
info@laxmipublications.com

Branches

	Branch	Telephone	
✆	Bangalore	080-26 75 69 30	
✆	Chennai	044-24 34 47 26,	24 35 95 07
✆	Cochin	0484-237 70 04,	405 13 03
✆	Guwahati	0361-254 36 69,	251 38 81
✆	Hyderabad	040-27 55 53 83,	27 55 53 93
✆	Jalandhar	0181-222 12 72	
✆	Kolkata	033-22 27 43 84	
✆	Lucknow	0522-220 99 16	
✆	Mumbai	022-24 91 54 15,	24 92 78 69
✆	Ranchi	0651-220 44 64	

C—
Printed at : Repro Knowledgecast Limited, Thane

To
Senanu Adika

CONTENTS

PREFACE

Deviant Usage and Confusing Words is a compilation of short articles published weekly in *The Heritage* from 2002–2004. *The Heritage* is a Ghanaian newspaper published by Heritage Communications Limited, Accra.

In the first edition, my objective was to sharpen the awareness of Educated English-speaking Ghanaians on deviant usage peculiar to English in Ghana and on commonly confused words. The objective remains the same for this new edition. However, this second edition has been expanded to include. 14 new articles which were written after the publication of the first edition. A new feature designed to increase the word power of users of the book is the "Dictionary Work" box at the end of each unit. The vocabulary items for study relate to the thematic focus of the unit, and are intended not only to augment the word power of the user but also to stimulate their dictionary use habit. It is common knowledge that many educated people especially those who do routine work hardly touch the dictionary.

As regards the original articles which comprised the first edition, minor revisions have been made to them to improve their content and quality of language. The unit on "Some Idiomatic Expressions" has been comprehensively expanded with a dictionary exercise on 50 idiomatic expressions. Also, a subject index has been included in this edition.

I would like to repeat from the preface to the first edition that the intended audience for this book are students, teachers, journalists and individuals desirous of improving their English. The book may be used as a quick reference material or it may be read from beginning to the end.

I wish to acknowledge the use I have made of various dictionaries and general reference sources. These sources I have listed in the bibliography.

I am grateful to the following people for various forms of support during the writing of the articles that constitute the material for the two editions of the book: Dr. Kwabena Duffour, Mr. Kofi Duffour, the late Professor S. A. Nkrumah, Mr. Michael Quarshie, Mr. Benedict Kyei Asante, Mr. Jonathan Lamptey, Ms. Dorothy Arhin and the late Justice Bakidamteh.

-Author

Part One
Grammar and Usage

1

British or American English?

Spelling

There are numerous varieties of the English language. We can speak of regional varieties, and varieties according to subject matter, medium and attitude. Most of us would have heard of or used the labels, Ghanaian English, Nigerian English, Canadian English, Indian English, etc. All these are regional varieties; and within these varieties there are varieties according to subject matter, medium and education. The most distinctive feature of regional varieties is pronunciation. In other words, it is relatively easy to recognize a regional variety on the basis of the speaker's pronunciation. Other features such as vocabulary and grammatical variation may be noticed later in the person's language of person.

In terms of written English, specifically spelling, all the regional varieties reflect a single system, with two minor subsystems: (a) the subsystem with British orientation and (b) the subsystem with American orientation. In Ghana, it has been the practice to follow British spelling norms. However, with the increasing use of the Internet and the widespread use of North American books brought into the country by Non-governmental Organisations (NGOs), students, teachers, and many other people constantly encounter American spelling. The effect of all this is the unwarranted mixture of British and American spelling in the same text. In one text, we may encounter **center** and **centre** (my computer just reminded me that centre is wrong and automatically changed it to center). Other examples are: 'color' and 'colour'; 'favourable' and 'favorable' etc.

I recognize the strength of the American influence; and can only appeal that we try to be consistent in our spelling. When you write, stick to one subsystem: either American or British. Do not mix the two. A few examples of differences between the two subsystems of spelling are as follows:

British Double 'l'	**American Single 'l'**
Counsellor	Counselor
Levelled	Leveled
Libellious	Libelous
Travelling	Traveling

British 'ae/oe'	**American 'e'**
Anaesthetist	Anethetist
Encyclopaedia	Encyclopedia
Amoeba	Ameba
Manoeuvre	Maneuvre
Foetus	Fetus

British 're'	**American 'er'**
Theatre	Theater
Metre	Meter
Spectre	Specter
Fibre	Fiber
Litre	Liter

British 'our'	**American 'or'**
Labour	Labor
Honour	Honor
Harbour	Harbor
Rancour	Rancor
Favour	Favor

Vocabulary

Vocabulary is one of the most dynamic areas of any language in that it is that part of a language that is constantly changing and expanding to reflect the knowledge, experience and spirit of the community that uses it. Historically, many American words have crept into the British English and they have been so completely absorbed by Britons that dictionaries do not think it important any longer to state the fact. However, there are still some vocabulary items that are uniquely American, and that set American English apart from British English. I have read humorous accounts of Americans who have visited Britain and have had communication difficulties because British 'chips' are American 'French fries' and American 'chips' are British 'crisps'.

In Ghana, most of us use some British and American words synonymously, generally out of a lack of awareness of the differences and, probably, because of the overwhelming American cultural influence today. I am neither proposing that we use purely British words nor am I saying that the use of the American words is wrong. Rather, I think the fact that we use some of these words interchangeably may be an indication of the gradual harmonization of British and American English, at least so far as vocabulary is concerned. For the sake of 'trouble-free' trips to Britain or America for international intelligibility, I would like to draw our attention to a few differences in vocabulary between British and American English. Comprehensive accounts of the distinction between the two varieties are provided in major dictionaries, grammar books and Internet sources.

British English	American English
Petrol	Gas
Motorway	Interstate
Pavement	Sidewalk
Car park	Parking lot
University	College
Exhibition	Exhibit
Courgette	Zucchini
Aubergine	Egg plant
Rubbish	Garbage
Dustbin	Trashcan
Flat	Apartment
Ground floor	First floor
Toilet	Restroom
Trousers	Pants

Dictionary Work

Study the meanings of the following American English expressions and find out (a) their levels of formality and (b) parallel expressions in British English:

1. *assisted living facility*
2. *I've got your back*
3. *cocooning*
4. *contingent worker*
5. *desk fast*
6. *pink slip party*
7. *drop dead date*
8. *face time*
9. *four-one-one (411)*
10. *mission creep*
11. *be termed out of office*

2

Is it a 'global world' or a 'globalized world'?

Language, it is said, reflects the spirit of the age. Indeed, many scholars have commented upon the relationship between the popularity of certain words and expressions and the changing face of society. These days it is not unusual to hear the words 'capacity building', 'fast track' (in different contexts of use), 'zero tolerance', not forgetting 'domestication' in the news, in political speeches and public debates[1]. A phrase that has caught my attention is 'global world'. Which is commonly used in public discourse in the Ghanaian media. But is this expression correct?

First, the word look at the meaning of 'world' since it's the qualified item. 'World' means 'the earth, together with all of its countries, and natural features', or 'all of the people, societies and institutions on earth'. What about the qualifier 'global'? 'Global' refers to 'the whole world', or simply 'worldwide', or 'the entire earth'. So when we talk about a 'global world' we are in effect saying 'a worldwide world', which to me is tautological. What is the essence of a qualifier? A qualifier restricts or extends the meaning of the word it modifies. Of course, for hyperbolical or exaggerated effects, tautologies may be excusable. However, I doubt whether the users of the phrase 'global world' have the rhetorical effect of hyperbole in mind.

I presume the origin of 'global world' is on analogy from 'global village'—a somewhat technical phrase[2]. This phrase is not tautological since it is a clear case of the use of the peculiar

† See Endnotes at the end of the book.

features of 'a village'—small, closely-knit, or integrated—to explain the integrative effects of worldwide telecommunications. Unfortunately, 'world' does not have that contrastive power. Flipping through an issue of the University of Ghana Campus Update (a newsletter), I came across this quote from the Vice Chancellor's Congregation 2002 address: 'We have trained your minds intellectually to meet the challenges of a complex and radically changing globalized world.' (Emphasis mine). This usage is correct. Let's the word take a look at the definition of 'globalized'. The word 'Globalized' means 'develop or be developed so as to make possible international influence or operation'. For example, 'Building facilities overseas is part of the strategy of every company that aims to globalize.'

So 'globalized' is more appropriate qualifier for word 'world' since it has a much more restrictive meaning capturing a development-oriented process which emphasizes operations and influences across national divisions. In other words, by semantic restriction the qualifier 'globalized' explains more clearly the interactive processes that affect the world. So the correct phrase is a 'globalized world'.

Dictionary Work

Study the meanings of the following words:

1. *universal*
2. *cosmopolitan*
3. *terrestrial*
4. *cosmical*
5. *exclusive*
6. *astronomical*

3

Which is correct: 'declared the meeting open/opened'?

Which of these two sentences is correct?

1. The chairman declared the meeting open at 10:55 a.m.
2. The chairman declared the meeting opened at 10:55 a.m.

Both sentences are semantically the same but grammatically Sentence (1) appears to be more acceptable.

Semantically, 'open' (adjective) and 'opened' (verb) have the same meaning, which is – 'ready to be used', 'ready to provide a service', or generally speaking, 'to begin to do something'. Examples:

3. The supermarket is open till 8:00 p.m.
4. The new hospital was declared open by the mayor.
5. The Olympic Games opened last week.

So from the semantic perspective both words 'open' and 'opened' can be used in the context in question. Grammatically speaking, however, 'open' (as an adjective) seems to be the preferred word for the verb 'declare'. In English, verbs determine the sentence elements that may follow them. For example, while transitive verbs require objects, intransitives do not but may optionally be followed by adverbs or adverbials.

The verb 'declare' has the following structural configurations:

a. Declare + that, as in: The chairman declared that the meeting was over.

b. Declare + quote, as in: The chairman declared: 'The meeting is over.'

c. Declare + object + (to be) noun or adjective, as in: The chairman declared the meeting (object) over (adjective).

On the basis of structural configuration (c), sentence (1) 'The chairman declared the meeting open at 10:55 a.m.' is the preferred one.

Dictionary Work

The following verbs have been classified as 'declare' verbs[3]:

1. *adjudge*	7. *fancy*	13. *suppose*
2. *adjudicate*	8. *find*	14. *think*
3. *assume*	9. *judge*	15. *warrant*
4. *avow*	10. *presume*	
5. *believe*	11. *profer*	
6. *confer*	12. *prove*	

Do a dictionary study of these verbs and learn their meanings as well as grammatical information provided about them.

† See Endnotes at the end of the book.

4

Tribe or Ethnicity?

A survey of the meanings of the word 'tribe' and its derivatives 'tribal' and 'tribalism' shows that they are used mainly in derogatory senses (expressive of low opinion). Indeed in contemporary contexts when 'tribe' is used to refer to a community living within a traditional society it is considered offensive since it is strongly associated with past attitudes of white colonialists towards so-called primitive or uncivilized people living in remote undeveloped places. Thus, is it not intriguing that many of us still use the word 'tribe' and its derivatives in reference to our places of origin?[4]

The word 'tribe' was not originally negative. In ancient Rome, it was used to refer to each of several political divisions; and each division was based essentially on a religious foundation. Each tribe had its common sacrifices and festivals and, most importantly, stood on equal terms with the other. However, a survey of the current usage of the word 'tribe' shows that it has shifted from its neutral sense and has adopted derogatory, hence negative associations.

Let's examine some of the meanings of 'tribe' and its derivatives; but let's remember that these senses are mainly derogatory.

'Tribe' is used to refer to a distinctive close-knit social or political group; or to a group or class of people or things. For

† See Endnotes at the end of the book.

example, 'Professor Mensah didn't want to be associated with the tribe of socialist theoreticians.' The adjective 'tribal' means concerning or characteristic of a tribe or tribes; or characterized by a tendency to form groups by strong loyalty. Example: 'Tribal affiliations at schools are not allowed'.

'Tribalism' refers to the state or fact of being organized in a tribe or tribes. It also refers to the behaviour and attitudes that stem from strong loyalty to one's own 'tribe' or social group. Example: 'Tribalism hinders national development.'

When referring to population subgroups or communities of people with one language and a common cultural tradition, it is generally preferable to use 'ethnic' or 'ethnicity'. Examples: 'We recruit our employees regardless of ethnic origins.'; 'She is from the Ewe ethnic group.'; 'The diverse experience of women of different ethnicities.'

Dictionary Work

Study the meanings of the following words:

1. *atavism*	8. *ethnocentric*
2. *avuncular*	9. *ethnography*
3. *fraternity*	10. *ethnomethodology*
4. *kindred*	11. *ethnoscience*
5. *phyletic*	12. *ethnic cleansing*
6. *sorority*	13. *ethnic minority*
7. *tribalist*	14. *ethnocide*

5

What is the difference between 'life history' and 'life story'?

An old school mistress always insisted that it was absolutely wrong to use the phrase 'life history' to refer to the events that have taken place in a person's life. She explained that the correct expression is 'life story'; and that 'life history' strictly refers to life cycle, that is, the history of the biological development of an organism. How accurate is this position?

For our answer, let's survey the definitions of 'life history' and 'life story' from a few dictionaries. The Webster's Seventh New Collegiate Dictionary published in 1967 defines life history as (1) a history of the changes through which an organism passes in its development from the primary stage to its natural death; and (2) the history of an individual's development in his social environment. In this dictionary, there is no separate entry for 'life story'. It is also not listed in the American Heritage Dictionary (1972, 1977) which defines 'life history' as 'an account of a person's life; a biography'. Thus of these two American dictionaries, one's definition of 'life history' covers both biological development and biography; while the other limits it to biography.

Let's consider some definitions from British-corpora based dictionaries. The Cambridge International Dictionary of English (1995) indicates that 'life history' is synonymous with either 'life cycle' or 'life story'. It gives the following explanation—'The life cycle or life history of a living thing is the series of changes it goes through from the beginning of its life until death'. For example, 'Perhaps the main event in the life cycle of a salmon is the return to its breeding grounds'. The dictionary further explains that 'A person's life history or life story is the series of events that they have lived through since their birth.' For example, 'The woman sitting next to me started to tell me her whole life history.' In the New Oxford Dictionary of English (1998), 'life history' is defined as (1) the series of changes undergone by an organism during its lifetime; and (2) the story of a person's life, especially when told at tedious length.

So far both the American and British dictionaries have used 'life history' to refer to both the biological development of an organism and the biographical information on a person. The only apparent contradiction is the definitions given by the 4th and 6th editions of the Oxford Advanced Learner's Dictionary (OALD) of Current English. The OALD (4th edition, 1989) makes the following distinction: 'life history' is used in a biological sense and refers to the record of the life cycle of an organism; while 'life story' refers to the provision of biographical information as in the sentence – 'She told me her life story'.

However in the 6th edition of the OALD (2000), the definition of 'life history' is extended to cover 'life story'. In this edition, 'life history' is defined as 'all the events that happen in the life of a person, animal or plant'. This more recent definition naturally overrides that of the 4th edition. It must be noted further that in the 6th edition, 'life story' is simply defined as 'the story that somebody tells you about their whole life' expunging the sense of factual neutrality that 'life history' carries.

Clearly, the position of the old school mistress is not fully tenable. 'Life history' can be used to refer to either the biographical information of a person or the biological development of an organism. So when writing or talking about people you can use the expression 'life history'.

What is the difference between 'life history' and 'life story'?

Dictionary Work

Study the meanings of the following words:

1. *autobiography*
2. *curriculum vitae*
3. *hagiography*
4. *memorabilia*
5. *memoirs*
6. *matyrology*

6

Money Talks

In most of its uses, 'money' has no plural, but when the reference is to discrete sums of money, usually obtained from various sources or distributed to various individuals or groups, the plural 'moneys' or 'monies' is often used (Merriam Webster 1989)[5]. Example: 'The project depended on community monies'.

Let's consider some expressions formed with 'money'. It must be noted, though that most of these expressions are either spoken or used informally. The meaning of the sentence is 'Pay good money for' means to spend a lot of money on something. Example: 'I paid good money for that briefcase, so take good care of it.' 'There's money (to be made) in' is used to say that you can get a lot of money from a particular activity or from buying and selling something. Example: 'There is money in selling food.'

If you say that someone 'has money to burn', you mean they have more money than they need or that they spend their money on things that you think are unnecessary. Example: 'Many businessmen have money to burn'.

'To get your money's worth' is to get something worth the price that you paid. Example: 'At that price you want to make sure you get your money's worth'. The expression 'money is no object' is used to say that you can spend as much money as you want to on something. Example: 'Choose whatever you like, money is no object'.

† See Endnotes at the end of the book.

'If you put your money where your mouth is' you show by your actions that you really believe what you say, or you support what you have said by risking or investing money, or giving other material or practical help. Example: 'Kofi has so much confidence in his wife's retail business that he has invested millions of cedis in it. Indeed he has put his money where his mouth is'.

Another useful expression is 'be rolling in money,' which means to be very rich. Example: 'They're always having parties; they must be rolling in money'.

'Money talks' is used to say that money is powerful, and people who have money can get what they want; or they have power and influence over others.

Associated with the use of money are the words 'change' and 'balance'. Their meanings are often confused. 'Change' is used for the amount of money that is given back to you when you have given more for something than the amount it costs. Example: 'You have to give me five cedis change.'

For example, if you have an amount of GH¢500 in your bank account and you withdraw GH¢100, your available balance is GH¢400. On the other hand, if you deposit GH¢100 your total balance will be GH¢600. In other words, 'balance' refers to the amount left after some money has been withdrawn from or deposited into your bank account. Do not use 'balance' to mean 'change' [6].

Dictionary Work

Study the meanings of the following words:

1. *hard currency*
2. *fiducial currency*
3. *depreciation currency*
4. *power of the purse*
5. *letter of credit*
6. *coin of the realm*

7

Chop-Chop

'Chop–Chop' is an informal expression meaning hurry-up: 'Chop–chop, we haven't got all day !' It originated from Pidgin English based on a Chinese dialect word for 'quick'. In the sense of 'hurry-up' the expression hardly occurs in English in Ghana, but it is used in sub-standard forms to refer to food or the act of eating[7].

So we have expressions such as 'Chop bar', 'chop-money' and so on. We need to note that 'chop' occurs in standard English usage, and its usage constitutes the material for discussion in this section.

As a verb, 'chop' as in 'chop something up' means to cut something into pieces with a sharp tool such as a knife. Examples: (1) 'Chop the carrots up into small pieces'. (2) 'He was chopping logs for firewood. There is also a figurative sense, which is 'to divide into smaller units'. Example: 'The country was chopped up into small administrative areas'.

'Chop' also means to reduce something by a large amount. This is synonymous with 'cut'. Example: 'The share price was chopped from GH¢5 to GH¢2'. Another meaning of 'chop' is to hit something with a short downward stroke or blow. Example: 'Kofi chopped the wild cat on the head'.

'To chop (away) at something' means to aim blows at something with a heavy sharp tool such as an axe. Example: 'He chopped away frantically at the log'. 'To chop something down'

† See Endnotes at the end of the book.

is to make something, such as a tree, fall by cutting it at the base with a sharp tool. Example: 'The gardener chopped the tree down with all his energy'.

'To chop something off (something) is to remove something by cutting with a sharp tool. Examples: (1) 'He chopped a branch off the tree'. (2) 'The executioner chopped off his head after the trial'.

'Chop and change' is an informal expression meaning to keep changing your mind or what you are doing. Example: 'I'm not surprised at Yaw's chop and change attitude'. The following words may be used as synonyms for 'chop and change' — 'shuffle' and 'be shifty'.

As a noun 'chop' refers to a thick slice of meat with a bone attached to it especially from a pig or sheep. Example: 'pork / lamb chop'. It also refers to the act of hitting something with the side of your hand in a quick downward movement. Example: 'a karate chop'.

The word 'chops' refers to the part of a person's or an animal's face around the mouth. Example: 'The dog started licking its chops'.

When you 'get or are given the chop', it means you have been dismissed from a job. Example: 'Mary was given the chop yesterday'. The expression may also be used in reference to a plan or a project being stopped. Example: 'Three more projects have got the chop'.

Dictionary Work

Study the meanings of the words listed under the different uses of 'chop':

1. *chop (cut): hack, cleave, decapitate*
2. *chop (piece): torso, chunk, splinter*
3. *chop (shorten): abbreviate, truncate, whittle*

8

Catch-22

A catch-22 situation has been defined as a situation in which a desired outcome or solution is impossible to attain because of a set of inherently illogical rules or conditions. In other words, it is an impossible situation where you are prevented from doing one thing until you have done another thing, but you cannot do the other thing until you have done the first thing.[8]

Some job advertisements offer career opportunities for young graduates make job experience a requirement for eligibility to apply. However, the reality is that having just finished school, most of these graduates have never been employed. Therefore, they find themselves in a catch-22 situation: they have not got experience so they cannot apply for the job and they cannot get experience until they first get a job. Let us now consider a few expressions formed with 'catch'.

'To catch up with' someone who has committed a crime or done something wrong means to succeed in finding them, especially in order to arrest or punish them. Example: 'The police will catch up with the highway robbers one day'.

If something catches up with you, you find yourself in an unpleasant situation, which you have been able to avoid until now but which you are now forced to deal with or accept responsibility for. For instance, this expression may be used for someone who is living a double life: he works as a messenger in

† See Endnotes at the end of the book.

a firm but tells his wife he is a clerk. So we can say—'The truth will catch up with him'.

Another commonly used expression is—'catch someone's eye' which means you do something to attract their attention, so that you can speak to them or ask them to do something. Example: 'Can you catch the policeman's eye?'; or 'He failed to catch the Speaker's eye in the Parliament yesterday'.

If you 'catch' an idea, a suggestion, or a hint, you understand the implications of what someone is saying. Example: 'You have to know the professor pretty well to catch all the allusions'.

'To catch sight of something or someone or 'catch a glimpse' of them is to suddenly notice them. Example: 'From her position she is able to catch sight of intruders'. We can also say—'Out of the corner of my eye I caught a glimpse of the ladies'.

If you are caught without something, you do not have it when you need it. Example: 'She always catches me without any sugar in the house'. This usage brings to mind the expression 'To catch somebody with their pants down', which means the people are unprepared to do what you have asked or you have caught them in an embarrassing situation. Example: 'John was caught with his pants down when the guests arrived. Dinner was not ready, and the snails meant for the meal were crawling all over the house'.

Dictionary Work

Study the meanings of the following words:

1. dilemma
2. dubiety
3. predilection
4. expedience
5. fastidiousness
6. cooptation

9

Touch Wood

'Touch wood' is a superstitious or humorous expression that is supposed to prevent bad luck, often people actually touch a piece of wood when they say it. Example: 'If on your journey in the night, touch wood, your car develops an engine problem, what will you do'. Probably the equivalent in local parlance is—'Taflatse'[9].

There are other beautiful expressions or phrases formed with 'touch'. These are: the common touch, in touch, out of touch, keep in touch, lose touch , touch off, touched and touchy.

'The common touch' is a person's natural ability to have a good relationship with ordinary people and be popular with them. Example: 'Even his enemies had to admit he had the common touch'. or 'He despised his fellow MPs for affecting the common touch'.

'In touch', means you have up-to-date information, knowledge, and understanding about something, or somebody. If you are out of touch with something, you no longer have this information, knowledge, or understanding. Example: 'I am helping the Government to stay in touch with the feelings of the minority'. or 'They seem incredibly out of touch with the reality of living in Accra'. If you keep in touch with someone, you write to them, telephone them, or visit them regularly so that you can exchange news.

---

† See Endnotes at the end of the book.

If you 'lose touch' with someone you gradually stop writing, telephoning, or visiting them. Example: 'We finally lost touch after she moved to London'. or 'You may lose touch with him if you don't take his number'.

If something 'touches off a situation or series of events, it causes it to start happening. Example: 'The police action touched off another night of rioting'.

If you say that someone is 'touched', you mean that they are slightly mad. Example: 'We thought she was a bit touched'. This is synonymous with 'batty' which means the person is rather eccentric or slightly mad.

'Touchy' may be used to describe a person or a subject. A touchy person is easily upset, offended or irritated. Example: 'He always was a touchy and quick-tempered man'. or 'They are touchy about criticism'. A touchy subject is one that needs to be dealt with carefully and tactfully because it might upset or offend people. Example: 'Security is a touchy subject among government officials at the moment'.

Dictionary Work

Study the meanings of the following words and expressions:

1. *soft touch*
2. *finishing touch*
3. *touch-me-not*
4. *touch-and-go*
5. *wouldn't touch something with a barge pole*
6. *touchstone*

10

Go to Pieces

In the 1970s, Jimmy Cliff's 'Go to Pieces' was a hit. I was a kid then but I still remember the melody with nostalgia. This unit focuses on the expression 'go to pieces' and others formed with 'pieces'.

If someone 'goes to pieces', they are so upset, frightened, or nervous that they can no longer do or cope with what they should do. It is a fairly informal expression. Example: 'John did not go to pieces when Mary jilted him'.

If someone tears you to pieces or pulls your work or ideas to pieces, they criticise your behaviour, your work, or your ideas very severely. This is an informal expression. Example: I explained my theory and he just pulled it to pieces.

The word 'piece' or 'pieces' is very useful when you wish to associate with singularity uncountable nouns like information, advice, news, music and so on. Examples: (1*a*) 'He gave me pieces of information'; (1*b*) 'He gave me a piece of information'; (2*a*) She gave me pieces of advice. (2*b*) 'She gave me a piece of advice'. It is wrong to say – 'an information' or 'an advice'. Rather you must say 'a piece of information' or 'a piece of advice'. The word 'some' may also be used in such contexts. So you can say – 'some information' or 'some advice'.

A piece is also something that is written or created. For example an article, play, or short musical composition. Example: 'An interesting piece about the religious leader'; 'I played the piece for 10,000 people'.

If something, for example a plan or system, is 'in pieces', it has been destroyed or is no longer useful or effective. Example: 'The company's strategy now lies in pieces destroyed by the government's new economic policy'. (in ruin; in shreds).

If something or someone is still 'in one piece', for example after a dangerous journey or experience, it is safe and not damaged, injured, or harmed. Example: 'Surprisingly, most of the crockery was still in one piece'.

If something with several different parts is 'all of a piece' it is the same throughout or consistent in some way. If one thing is 'of a piece' with another, it is consistent with it. This usage is fairly formal.

When you say your piece, you say what to say about a particular matter. Example: 'Right, now I've said my piece, I'll sit down'.

If you piece together the truth about something or the nature or meaning of something, you gradually discover it or understand it by becoming aware of different facts or by considering how they fit together. Examples: (1) 'I found out the truth by piecing together hints and rumours that I heard at school'. (2) 'She had not yet been able to piece together exactly what had happened'.

The word 'piece' is also used in the following expressions—'bits and pieces', 'a piece of cake'; 'to give someone a piece of your mind'; 'to pick up the pieces'.

Dictionary Work

Study the meanings of the following words:

1. *piecemeal*
2. *piecework*
3. *piecegoods*
4. *holistic*
5. *seamless*
6. *corpus*

11

Ring Road

The word 'ring road' is documented as coming into the English language in 1928, (Ayto 1999): 'London has no form, no symmetry. I suggest that we could give her this by cutting a broad ring-road through the old nineteenth century suburbs'. (The Daily Express) 'Ring road' thus came to mean a by-pass road encircling a town or other urban area. In American English, 'ring road' is referred to as 'beltway' (ca.1951). Though there is also the word "belt highway' (1945), 'beltway' is the much more common expression. In Accra, the road that runs in front of the Ghana Broadcasting Corporation all the way to the Nkrumah Circle is referred to as the ring road, with associated links like– ring road west, ring road east and so on.

What about the word 'by-pass'? 'By-pass' came into the language in 1922 as documented by the Daily Mail: 'New roads and by-passes, which should remove some of the danger spots'. It is in a way synonymous with 'ring-road'. Additionally, it is often used in reference to alternative routes which are created when major roads are being reconstructed.

There is also the word 'detour' which means an alternative route for use by traffic when the usual road is temporarily closed. So when you use a by-pass you could be making a detour.

Another meaning of 'detour' is a long or roundabout route that is taken to avoid something or to visit somewhere along the way: 'He makes a detour to an internet cafe on his way to work on Mondays'. A 'detour' may also be explained as a way of going from one place to another that is longer than the usual way, for example because you want to avoid traffic problems or to visit something. The expression is 'to make/take a detour'. Of course, it is also used as a verb with the meaning to take a long or roundabout route. Example: 'He detoured around the market'.

Now, let's examine other expressions formed with the word 'ring'.

'Ring-fence' is to make an official decision that something, especially money, can only be used for a particular purpose. Example: 'We need to ring-fence ¢10 million as funds for the road project'. It may also be used to mean guarantee that funds allocated for a particular purpose will not be spent on anything else. Example: 'The financial manager of the company failed to ring-fence the money provided for downsizing'. The word also means guard securely or protect as in: 'The workers are attempting to ring-fence their jobs'.

'Ring hollow' is used to refer to words that you feel are untrue or insincere. Example: 'The manager's expression of remorse rang hollow'. The expression 'have a ring of truth" means seems likely to be true. Example: 'The story of the accused has a ring of truth about it'.

'Ring the changes' means to make changes to something, not because it needs changing but just in order to make it more interesting or more attractive. Example: 'You may ring the changes in your car by polishing the dashboard and changing the seat covers'. The expression also means to do something in many different ways; or to say or wear the same thing in different ways. Example: 'This month Mr. Mensah has rung the changes with three shirts and two pairs of trousers'.

The word 'ring-pull' was first used in the English language in 1970 to denote a seal on a drink can which is broken by pulling a ring attached to it. As a noun, it is used to refer to the ring itself. These days some types of canned fish or food (even on the Ghanaian market) have a 'ring-pull'. So we can talk of a 'ring-pull can'.

Dictionary Work

Study the meanings of the following words:

1. *fairway*
2. *viaduct*
3. *gangway*
4. *trajectory*
5. *turnpike*
6. *artery*

12

Rack Your Brains!

The brain refers to the organ inside the skull head that controls movement, thought, memory and feeling. In English, several expressions or phrases are formed with the word 'brain(s)'. Most of these relate to intelligence or lack of it. When the word 'brain' is used it refers to intelligence, it means 'the ability to learn quickly' and think about things in a logical and intelligent way as exemplified by the following sentences: (1) It doesn't take much brain to work out that both stories can't be true. (2) Teachers spotted that he had a good brain at an early age. The expression 'You need brains as well as brawn.' means 'You need intelligence as well as strength'.

'Brains' can also be used to refer to an intelligent person. Note that in this usage, 'brains' is a plural noun. It may therefore be used for one person or more. In the sentence—'We have the best scientific brains in the country working on the project.', the word 'brains' refers to intelligent scientists. There is also the phrase 'the brains' which is used to refer to 'the most intelligent person in a particular group or the person who is responsible for thinking of and organizing something'. For instance, you can say, (1) 'He's always been the brains of the family'; (2) 'The marketing manager is the brains behind the company's latest product'.

Other useful words formed with 'brain' are: brainstorm, brainstorming, brain drain, brainwash and brainchild. In British English, 'brainstorm' as a noun refers to a sudden inability to think clearly which causes unusual behaviour, as in the sentence 'She had a brainstorm in the exam and didn't answer a single question'. In American English, a 'brainstorm' means a 'brainwave' or 'a sudden good idea'. 'Brainstorming' refers to a way of making a group of people all think about something at the same time, often in order to solve a problem or to create good ideas. So we can say, 'a brainstorming session'.

Below are the meanings of some words formed with 'brain'. 'Brain drain' refers to the movement of highly skilled and qualified people to a country where they can work in better conditions and earn more money. 'Brainwash' means to force somebody to accept your ideas or beliefs for example by repeating the same thing many times or by preventing the person from thinking clearly. For instance, we can say—'The group is accused of brainwashing its young members'. 'Brainchild' refers to an idea or invention of one person or a small group of people.

In Ghana, people sometimes use the expression—'crack your brains'. Now, do you 'rack' or 'crack' your brains? The correct expression is 'rack your brains', and it means to think very hard for a long time about something. So you can say—'She racked her brains, trying to remember what the chairman said at the meeting'. There is also the form 'wrack', but this is less frequent. People generally use the spelling 'rack'.

Dictionary Work

Study the meanings of the following words:

1. brain	*5. brain trust*
2. damage	*6. brainless*
3. brain-dead	*7. brainpower*
4. brain death[10]	*8. brain-teaser*

† See Endnotes at the end of the book.

13

Do I mean every two months or twice a month?

As a language teacher, students and professionals have persistently questioned me on the differences in meaning between 'biannual' and 'biennial', and on the exact meaning of 'bimonthly' and 'biweekly'. Of course, the obvious starting-point for my response is to explain that the prefix 'bi-' means 'two' or 'twice'. So 'bimonthly', for instance, means 'every two months' or 'twice a month'. People are quick to point out the vast difference between the two meanings. How could they tell which meaning the writer or the speaker had in mind?

These concerns are by no means limited to the Ghanaian English usage context. Indeed, according to the Merriam-Webster's Dictionary of English Usage, editors of the dictionary receive many letters about time words formed with the prefix 'bi-', especially 'bimonthly' and 'biweekly'. People are outraged or distressed that 'bimonthly', for example, may mean either 'every two months' or 'twice a month'. The dictionary gives us a historical account of how, over the years, people have been using these words in two different ways. The result? These meanings have come to stay, or to put it in linguistic terms, have become 'standardized'.

So how do we resolve cases of ambiguity? First let's note the following dictionary definitions of 'bimonthly', 'biannual', and 'biennial'. 'Bimonthly' (as already explained above) means occurring or produced twice a month or every two months.

For instance, we can have a 'bimonthly newsletter'; which means the newsletter is published two times in a month or after every two months. 'Biannual' means occurring twice a year. Therefore, you can say 'the biannual meeting of the planning committee' which means the committee meets twice a year. 'Biennial' means taking place every other year. For example, the sentence—'Summit meetings are normally biennial', means the meetings are held every two years.

In cases of ambiguity, it is always helpful to provide your audience with sufficient information; that is, information that would indicate clearly to them that you are using 'bi-' in a specific sense: either to mean, for example, 'twice a week' or 'every two weeks'. For instance, you can say: 'Our bi-weekly newspaper is published on Tuesdays and Fridays'; where you are referring to twice a week. And 'Our bi-weekly newspaper is published in the second and fourth weeks of the month', in the case of every two weeks.

So the solution to the ambiguity presented in the 'bi-' time words discussed may be summarized as follows: If you find yourself in a situation where only a bi-word will do, you should give your audience sufficient contextual information as to your intended meaning. Additionally, you can use alternative expressions like 'every two months' and 'twice a month'.

Dictionary Work

Study the meanings of the following words:

1. *quinquennial*
2. *decennial*
3. *centennial*
4. *epochial*
5. *millennial*
6. *perennial*

14

'Paper' and 'Papers': When do we use the plural form?

Some people are unsure about the correct usage of the countable and uncountable forms of 'paper'[11]. Let's examine this problem.

When 'paper' is used to mean material for writing or wrapping, it is uncountable which means that the rules regarding uncountable nouns apply. Such rules as not adding an 's' to the word to signify plurality, and not using it with the indefinite article 'a'. It is therefore wrong to say—'I need a paper to write on', or 'I need to buy papers for the office'. Simply say, 'I need paper to write on' or 'I need to buy paper for the office'. If you have to indicate number especially in situations where you need to draw attention to quantity you can use 'paper' in combination with unit words such as 'piece, sheet, bundle and carton', in which case the 's' is added to the unit words and not to paper: pieces of paper, sheets of paper, bundles of paper, cartons of paper and so on. Note that the following words do not have the plural form—*notepaper, writing paper* and *wrapping paper.*

In its countable form, the word 'paper' can be used to refer to a newspaper. In this sense, you can associate it with singularity or plurality. For instance, we can have—'a local newspaper' or 'local newspapers', and 'I would like to buy two newspapers'. We can use the plural form 'papers' to refer to newspapers in general. So you can say—'The papers soon got hold of the story'.

Another example of the countable use of paper is in reference to an academic article about a particular subject that is written by

† See Endnotes at the end of the book.

and for specialists. For example, 'A recent paper in the Journal of Science', or 'recent papers in the Journal of Science', and 'She was invited to give a paper (a talk) on the results of her research', or 'She gave two papers at the conference', Furthermore, 'paper' also refers to a set of examination questions on a particular subject, and the answers that students write to the questions. For example, you can say—'The Maths paper was hard' or 'she spent the evening marking exam papers'.

Finally, the plural form 'papers' is used to refer to official or private documents. When a policeman stops you and asks for your papers he is referring to your car's documents. Documents concerned with divorce or identification may also be referred to as papers.

Dictionary Work

Study the meanings of the following words:

1. *papyrus*
2. *paper knife*
3. *paper thin*
4. *paper trail*
5. *papier-mache*
6. *paperweight*

15

Should we shun 'impact' as a verb?

The use of 'impact' (pronounced/impakt/) as a noun in a figurative sense is well established, and no longer stirs controversy. However, its use as a verb (pronounced/impakt/) in a figurative sense attracts adverse criticisms from certain quarters. We shall examine the meanings of 'impact' as a noun and then consider the criticisms of its use as a verb.

'Impact' as a noun means the action of one object coming forcibly into contact with another. Example: 'There was the sound of a third impact'. Figuratively, it means the effect or influence of one person, thing, or action on another. Example: 'The government's policies have had a significant impact on unemployment'.

Criticisms of the use of 'impact' as a verb in a figurative sense date from the early 80s. A fairly recent critic is Richard Marius (1995). In his book, *A Writer's Companion,* which is quite popular among journalism students in Ghana, he vehemently objects to the use of 'impact' as a verb. He remonstrates '... of late, impact has become a universal synonym for 'influence'. Polls impact elections. Reform movements impact welfare programs. Such usage is only another corruption of language spread by bureaucrats so uncertain of their own place in the world that they must devise strong-sounding language to convey the impression that they are doing more important tasks than, in fact, they are. Shun 'impact' as a verb. It is a neologism of the worst and most pretentious sort'. My question is—should we really shun 'impact' as a verb?

The assumption in Marius' assertion, and this notion underlies most of the criticisms on the use of 'impact' as a verb, is that it is derived from the noun by functional shift. But functional shift or conversion, as noted by The Oxford Companion to the English Language (1992), has for centuries been a common means of extending the resources of English and creating dramatic effects. So that is not sufficient justification for disapproving the use of the word. Interestingly, The Merriam Webster's Dictionary of English Usage (1989) points out that "impact" was a verb in English before it was a noun. It substantiates this claim with the explanation that the verb form is first attested in 1601 and was brought in straight from the past participle of the Latin verb that gave the English language "impinge". The book further explains that the figurative uses of the verb are parallel to, though no doubt influenced by the figurative sense of the noun, which is not a case of a verb derived from an earlier noun[12].

The Merriam Webster's Dictionary of English Usage cites a variety of sources to illustrate the figurative senses of the verb 'impact' to show that the usage is now standard and well established. Let's now examine the meanings of 'impact' as a verb. As a verb, 'impact' means come into forcible contact with. Example: 'The shell impacts fifty metres away'. Another meaning is to have a strong effect. Example: 'High interest rates will impact on private investment'. Additionally, 'to impact' means to press firmly. Example: 'The animals' feet do not impact and damage the soil as cows' hooves do'.

So we should not shun the use of 'impact' as a verb. However, as The Merriam Webster's Dictionary of English Usage admonishes, you need not use this verb if you find it unappealing since there are substitutes such as 'affect', 'influence', 'impinge' or 'hit' depending on the context.

---

† See Endnotes at the end of the book.

Dictionary Work

Study the meanings of the following words:

1. *invigorate*
2. *inebriate*
3. *induce*
4. *precipitate*
5. *benumb*
6. *stagnate*

16

Some Idiomatic Expressions

The term 'idiomatic' is derived from 'idiom' which means a group of words whose meaning is different from the meanings of the individual words. An idiomatic expression is, thus, an expression that contains an idiom.

It is naturally difficult to simply look at the individual words which constitute an idiomatic expression, and on the basis of that, tell the meaning of the expression. Idiomatic expressions are natural to native speakers of a language. In second language contexts, we typically find situations where the idiom is modified either by lexical change (*i.e.*, some of the words that constitute the idiom are substituted with others), or structural change (*i.e.*, the sequence of words is modified). Let us remind ourselves of the meanings and usage of some idiomatic expressions.

Have your cake and eat it too

The original version of the above mentioned idiom was 'You can't eat your cake and have it too'. This version is logical and is easily interpretable. Once you eat your cake, it is impossible to be in possession of it again. However, the reversed version 'You can't have your cake and eat it too'—has gained remarkable prevalence to the extent that many people are unsure as to which version is the more acceptable form. Indeed, many dictionaries today cite the reversed version as the proper form of the idiom. Ben Zimmer in an article in The New York Times (February 18, 2011, NYTimes.com) provides a fascinating account of the history behind the reversal and argues that swapping the verbs 'eat' and 'have' do not really affect the interpretation or meaning of the idiom. The use of 'and' to link the two verb phrases, he explains, should not 'imply a chronological sequence of events' but instead 'suggest that the two activities of having and eating cannot occur simultaneously'. I find the explanation convincing enough and in the light of the predominance of the usage of the reversed version among educated users of English coupled with the acceptability it has gained from dictionary entries I would recommend the use of 'You can't have your cake and eat it too'.

Let's now move from the structure of the idiom to its meaning. The idiom means to have or do two things at the same time that are impossible to have or do at the same time. A typical context in which this expression may be used is as follows: You have been given a scholarship to the United Kingdom for a one-year study programme; then you also get a prestigious award for a three-month study programme in the United States of America. However, the American award requires you to return to your home country for a period of six months to do community service. Therefore, if you accept the American award it would be impossible for you to also accept the scholarship to the UK. A friend may advise you thus: 'You can't have your cake and eat it. So take the scholarship to the UK and decline the American offer'.

Follow in somebody's footsteps

This means to do the same job or have the same style of life as somebody else, especially somebody in your family. For example, if John's father worked as an insurance officer and John also goes into that profession someone can say: 'John works in insurance, following in his father's footsteps'. Note that the expression is not 'follow somebody's footstep' but 'follow in somebody's footsteps'.

Be up to your neck in something

This means to have a lot of something to deal with. If the company you work for keeps on borrowing money to do business without making enough money to pay off the debts, you can say 'we're up to our neck in debt'.

The odd man/one out

This refers to a person or thing that is different from others or does not fit easily into a group or set. For example, (1) 'At school he was always the odd man out'. (2) 'Dog, cat, horse, shoe—which is the odd one out?'. In example 2, "shoe" does not fit in since all the others are four legged animals.

To conclude when you come across an idiomatic expression go for your dictionary and check its exact meaning. Study the words that form the idiom carefully. This will enable you to remember and use the idiomatic expression correctly.

Dictionary Work

Study the meanings of the following idiomatic expressions:

1. *make a song and dance about something*
2. *an ace up your sleeve*
3. *not know somebody from Adam*
4. *keep up appearance*
5. *have something on good authority*
6. *throw the baby out with the bath-water*
7. *have eyes in the back of your head*
8. *turn up like a bad penny*
9. *scrape the bottom of the barrel*
10. *more than you can shake a stick at*
11. *biological clock is ticking away*
12. *make all the correct noises*
13. *a heavy cross to bear*
14. *you could cut the atmosphere with a knife*
15. *be between the devil and the deep blue sea*
16. *like a dose of salts*
17. *just what the doctor ordered*
18. *go back to the drawing board*
19. *your ears must be burning*
20. *fray around/at the edges*
21. *have a memory like an elephant*
22. *chalk something up to experience*
23. *damn somebody with faint praise*
24. *a fair crack of the whip*
25. *be all fingers and thumbs*
26. *cut the ground from under somebody's feet*
27. *give somebody a dose/taste of their own medicine*
28. *take (or pick) up the gauntlet*
29. *go against the grain*
30. *hit the ground running*
31. *cross somebody's hand/palm with silver*
32. *run round like a headless chicken*

Dictionary Work

33. *wild horses wouldn't drag me*
34. *the milk of human kindness*
35. *put your heart and soul into something*
36. *I'll be a monkey's uncle*
37. *put ideas into somebody's head*
38. *get into the swing of it/things*
39. *go and take a running jump*
40. *cheque book journalism*
41. *keep up with the Joneses*
42. *pervert the course of justice*
43. *keep a civil tongue in (your) head*
44. *a different kettle of fish*
45. *blast/blow somebody/something to kingdom come*
46. *school of hard knocks*
47. *be laughing all the way to the bank*
48. *the blind leading the blind*
49. *leave a bad taste in (your) mouth*
50. *be like a red rag to a bull*

Part Two

Homophones and Confusing Words

17

Homophones and Confusing Words: An Introduction

Homophones refer to words which are pronounced the same as other words but have different meanings or different spellings or both. Let's consider the following words:

'Cue' /kju:/ meaning a word or action in a play or film, which is used as a signal by a performer to begin saying or doing something. 'Queue' /kju:/ referring to a line of people, usually standing and waiting for something. The words 'cue' and 'queue' have different spellings and meanings but their pronunciation is same – /kju:/

Closely associated with homophones are homographs. Homographs refer to words spelt the same as other words and might be pronounced the same or differently, but have different meanings. For example,

'Refuse' /rifju:z/ (verb) meaning to say no or turn down.

'Refuse' /rɛfju:s/ (noun) meaning waste, garbage or trash.

In everyday language use, we come across homophones and homographs and the confusion they sometimes create. Part two deals with some of these confusing occurrencies. It highlights the features that set them apart and provides examples of contexts in which they are used so that differences in usage of these confusing words can be better appreciated.

18

Back up and Buck up

The impression one gets listening to many Ghanaian speakers of English is that the distinction between the vowels /æ/ and /ʌ/ as in 'man' and 'must' is barely perceptible. Often the vowel sounds in such words are realised as the low mid vowel quality /a/. A colleague who is a phonetician argues that in the absence of socio-phonetic study of this phenomenon, there is no empirical basis for such a claim to be made[13]. Be that as it may, the tendency seems pervasive and it is worth drawing people's attention to it, lest we slip into situations where some individuals will use 'back up' to mean 'to encourage or become encouraged' instead of using the right spelling 'buck up'.

Back up

To back up /bækʌp/ a claim or story means to supply evidence to prove it is true. In other words, to support or substantiate the claim. Example: 'The chairperson always backs up his claims with statistics and weird theories'.

To back someone up means to give them help and support when they are in a difficult situation. Example: 'This is the time for us to back up our relatives in the villages'. The expression may also be used to mean to confirm what somebody is saying. Example: 'John felt he had to back Sarah up when everybody else doubted her story'.

In the context of driving, if you back up it means you reverse the vehicle. Example: 'I backed up a few metres to allow the other car to move'. You could also use the expression to mean to

† See Endnotes at the end of the book.

walk backwards a little way. Example: 'Kwame backed up slowly and then sprang forward'.

The noun form 'back-up' means help or support from people or machines, without which you would not be able to achieve what you want. Example: 'You need a back-up team for the project'. In military contexts, 'back-up' means reinforcement. Example: 'For rescue operations you always need back-up'. Note that 'back-up' is an uncountable noun. So you cannot say 'a back-up'; and you should not use it in the plural form.

Buck up

The word 'buck'/bʌk/ is said to have come into the English language around 1908 (Ayto 1999). The noun form 'the buck' means responsibility as used in the expression 'pass the buck' which means to shift blame, especially in a situation where you are responsible. Example: 'Don't pass the buck, Sir. You should have checked the machine before operating it'.

Another expression formed with 'buck' which is attributed to US President Harry Truman is 'the buck stops here'. This is used to mean it is your responsibility to deal with a particular problem especially in a situation where your subordinates have refused to accept the responsibility.

To buck someone up means to encourage them to be more cheerful. Example: 'The secretary looks downcast we need to buck her up'. 'Buck up' also means to hurry up. Example: 'Buck up, we will miss the bus'.

Dictionary Work

Study the meanings of the following words:

1. *buck naked*
2. *buck skin*
3. *buckteeth*
4. *backlash*
5. *backchat*
6. *backbench*

19

Cause and Course

In the following sentence, is the correct word 'cause' or 'course'? 'Thousands of workers demonstrated for the cause/course of freedom and justice'. We shall answer this question at the end of this piece.

Cause

The basic meaning of 'cause' (as a noun) is the reason why something happens, as used in the sentence—'The manager decided to investigate the cause of the strike action'. 'Cause' also means a socially valuable principle which is strongly supported by some people. Note, for example, this line from the national anthem of Ghana: 'Bold to defend forever the cause of freedom and of right'. There are other derivative nouns, e.g., 'causality' and 'causation'. 'Causality' refers to the principle that there is a cause for everything that happens; while 'causation' is the process of causing something to happen.

As a verb, 'cause' means to make something happen. Example: 'Bad roads cause accidents'. Note the adjective 'causal', which means a relationship or link between two things in which one causes the other. For example, 'There is a causal relationship between cigarette smoking and lung cancer'.

Course

As students, teachers and professionals, we have frequently used 'course' to refer to a plan of study usually resulting in an exam or qualification as in the sentence: 'Has he completed his English course?' 'Course' may also be used to describe the direction in which a vehicle, especially an aircraft, spacecraft or ship moves, or the path along which a river flows. Example: 'The lost hunters decided to follow the course of the river'. If something is on course it means it is likely to happen or likely to succeed as planned: 'The board has approved the budget so the restructuring is on course'.

'Course' is also used to refer to the gradual development of something, or the way something happens, or a way of doing something. Take note of the following illustrative sentences: (1) 'The course of the MP's campaign was marred by allegations of corruption in the press'. (2) 'What would be the appropriate course of action if you discovered your sixteen-year old daughter was pregnant?' (3) 'If your friends are spending more of their time at restaurants you don't have to follow the same course'. (4) 'The judge was accused of attempting to pervert the course of justice'.

The expressions 'during the course of' and 'in the course of' mean 'during' as used in the sentence: 'In the course of the crisis many of the employees resigned from the company'. 'In the course of time' means after a period of time as used in the example: 'The company plans to expand in the course of time'. It can also be used to mean gradually as in: 'In the course of time the children learnt to live with their stepmother'. 'With the course of time' is perfectly acceptable in such contexts.

I believe it is now apparent that the correct word for the sentence in the opening paragraph of this article is 'cause'. 'Cause' depicts a reason or a basis for action or belief, or a tenet while 'course' conveys a sense of duration, process or flow of human action, direction or development. So the sentence should read: 'Thousands of workers demonstrated for the cause of freedom and justice'.

Dictionary Work

Study the meanings of the following words:

1. *determinant*
2. *progenitor*
3. *leverage*
4. *inverteracy*
5. *curriculum*
6. *disquisition*

20

The Treachery of 'Casual'

It never crossed my mind for a second that 'causal' and 'casual' could be bedfellows till in one of my weekly newspaper articles entitled 'Cause and Course' my fingers mysteriously keyed in 'casual' in the phrase: 'causal relationship'. The irony of the matter is that my column had devoted itself to 'pontificating!' on the need for language users to be mindful of homographs and homonyms; to wit, words that are similar in spelling but different in pronunciation; and words that are similar in pronunciation but different in spelling. So what went wrong?

From a computer keyboard perspective the difference between 'causal' and 'casual' is simply the ordering of the letters 's' and 'u': 'us' for 'causal' and 'su' for 'casual'. Thus a little fidgeting of the fingers would smuggle in either word regardless of the context, with the computer smugly silent on your mistake.

Beyond the typographical slippery zone, let's deal with the differences of meaning between 'causal relationship' and 'casual relationship'. A 'causal relationship' is a link between two things in which one causes the other. For example: 'There is a causal relationship between cigarette smoking and lung cancer'. A 'casual relationship' on the other hand refers to a link or association that is not serious as in the sentence: 'Kwame has a casual relationship with Ama'. In its qualifier function, the word 'casual' is used in a general sense to mean not serious or done by chance. Examples: (1) 'The manager made casual remarks about his secretary's competence but she took them seriously'. (2) 'The policeman took a casual glance at the drunken men and continued on his beat'. (3) 'The museum is not open to casual visitors'.

'Casual' also means not formal and unsuitable for special occasions as in 'You don't wear casual clothes to a wedding reception'. Another meaning of 'casual' is temporary (note NOT temporal): 'Management considered engaging casual workers to clean the entire building'.

Note the words 'causality' and 'casualty' which could easily suffer from the typographical mistake described above. 'Causality' refers to the principle that there is a cause for everything that happens. 'Casualty' refers to a person injured or killed in a serious accident or war. Example: 'There were no casualties in the motor accident'.

As I typed this piece my fingers mixed up the spellings of the words at issue and I struggled hard to keep my eyes wide-open to deal with the treachery of 'casual'. Remember the computer does not always help in such instances; so when using words liable to typing slips sharpen your editorial knives and keep your eyes open.

Dictionary Work

Study the meanings of the following words:

1. *contingent*
2. *fluky*
3. *fortuitous*
4. *effectual*
5. *seminal*
6. *germinal*

21

Cease and Seize

There are differences in pronunciation and meaning between 'cease' and 'seize'. 'Cease' is pronounced /si:s/ while 'seize' is pronounced /si:z/. So in pronunciation 'cease' ends with a 's-s-s' sound while 'seize' ends with a 'z-z-z' sound. Let's consider differences in meaning between the two words.

Cease /si:s/

'Cease' means to stop happening or existing, or to stop something from happening or existing. The following sentences may be used to illustrate this meaning: (1) 'John's visits ceased after the accident'. (2) 'The workers voted to cease strike action immediately'. In military contexts, we often hear the expression—'The rebel leader ordered his men to cease fire;' which means he asked his men to stop shooting. There is the noun form 'ceasefire' which refers to a time when enemies agree to stop fighting, usually while a way is found to end the fighting permanently: 'The president was negotiating with the rebel leader for a ceasefire'.

We also have the noun form 'cessation' pronounced /seseiʃən/which means a pause in something. For example: 'Ghana called for an immediate cessation of hostilities'.

Seize /si:z/

One of the meanings of 'seize' is to suddenly take hold of something or somebody, using force. In this sense, it is synonymous with 'grab' as in: 'Kwame tried to seize the knife from the thief'. Another meaning of 'seize' is to take control of a place or situation, often suddenly and violently as in: 'The soldiers seized the airport at dawn'. A few years ago the expression – 'The army has seized control of the country'. was common in Africa. Another example is – 'He seized power in a military coup'. Take note of these other meanings of 'seize': (1) 'to arrest or capture somebody'—For example: 'The criminals were seized as they ran out of the house'. (2) 'To be quick to make use of a chance or an opportunity. In this sense it is also synonymous with 'grab': 'The party seized the initiative with both hands'. (quickly and with enthusiasm) (3) 'To affect somebody suddenly and deeply': 'Panic seized her'.

There is also the phrasal verb—'seize on/upon something', which means to suddenly show a lot of interest in something, especially because you can use it to your advantage. It is similar in meaning to 'pounce on/upon': 'The rumours were eagerly seized upon by the local press'. Additionally, we have the phrasal verb 'seize up' which refers to the parts of a machine not moving or not working properly: 'The engine suddenly seized up'. In Ghana, most of us would say—'The engine has seized'. This is incorrect. You have to add the particle 'up' to yield the correct form—'The engine has seized up'.

Note the noun form 'seizure' pronounced / si:ʒə / which may be used in the countable and uncountable sense, and refers to the use of legal authority to take something from somebody as in: 'The CEPS boss ordered the seizure of cocaine at the airport'. We can also have—'The army's seizure of power is wrong.', meaning the act of using force to take control of the country.

Dictionary Work

Check the meanings of the following words:

1. moratorium	*4. expropriate*
2. armistice	*5. divestment*
3. stalemate	*6. sequestration*

22

Censor and Censure

'Censor' and 'censure' can be distinguished on the basis of the pronunciation of their last syllables and in terms of meaning. 'Censor' is pronounced / sɛnsə / while 'censure' is pronounced /sɛnʃə/: Both words connote a sense of disapproval especially from the perspective of the affected party. Do not confuse 'censor' with 'censer' (ends in 'er') which refers to the container in which incense is burnt.

Censor

There is an interesting piece of history regarding the meaning of 'censor'. In ancient Rome, 'a censor' referred to a magistrate who took the census (a registration or count of citizens and their property to determine tax), supervised the conduct of citizens, and gave out public contracts. Naturally, some ordinary Romans would have considered this role disreputable. My guess then is that some of this negative association has remained in the use of the word today.

A censor, as used now, refers to a person who has been officially appointed by a government to examine plays, books, films, etc., and cut out or ban any parts of it that are considered to be immoral, usually according to the instructions of the government. The process typically involves removing anything that is considered offensive, morally unacceptable, or politically dangerous. Examples: (1) 'The ministry has set-up a committee to censor all romantic films'. (2) 'The censor did not like the response of film directors to his scheme of evaluation'.

Take note of the adjective 'censorious' pronounced /sɛnsɔ:rɪəs/ and the noun 'censorship' pronounced /sɛnsəʃɪp/. 'Censorious' is used to describe the thinking or behaviour of people who disapprove strongly of other people's actions and criticize them. In other words, someone who is censorious is always looking for mistakes and faults in other people and wanting to criticize them. You may also refer to such a person as a 'fault-finder'. Example: 'The employees were censorious of the Chief Executive Officer'.

'Censorship' refers to the practice or policy of censoring materials especially by government officials. Example: 'Many people were against the censorship of news from the conflict area'.

Censure

'Censure' pronounced /sɛnʃə/ means strong disapproval or condemnation of something that has been done, or of the way it was done. Example: 'The Town Council is of the view that past chairpersons of the council should be immune to censure'.

If you censure someone, you tell them that you strongly disapprove of them or of their actions. Example: 'The director censured the secretary's handling of the issue'. Take note of the following derivations: 'censurability' meaning being censurable, and 'censurable' meaning deserving censure or blamable.

Dictionary Work

Check the meanings of the following words:

1. censorate	*3. censorial*
2. censorian	*4. censoriable;*

Compare them with:

5. censurer	*7. censurability*
6. censurable	

23

Cite, Site and Sight

The interesting thing about the words 'cite', 'site' and 'sight' is that they have the same pronunciation: /sait/. So it is very easy to confuse them especially in written contexts. We shall take each word in turn and explain it, with the hope that you will not confuse them in future.

Cite

'Cite' is a verb and it means to mention something as a reason or an example to support what you are saying. For example: 'Yaw cited his friend's'inability to keep a secret as the reason for their strained relationship'. Another meaning is to speak or write the exact words from a book or an author. Example: 'The teacher cited a passage from Achebe's *Things Fall Apart*'. In legal language, 'cite' means to officially request somebody to appear in a court of law; or to subpoena the person. Example: 'The man was cited for contempt of court'. Additionally, 'cite' means to mention somebody officially or publicly because they deserve special praise: 'The policeman was cited for bravery in the battle with the armed robbers'.

Site

The word 'site' refers to a place where a building or town is situated: 'I'm going to the construction site', or 'The government has a new site for the zoo'. 'Site' may also be used to mean a place where something has happened or that is used for something. For example, 'The site of an accident'. In computing, it refers to a place on the Internet where an organisation puts information: 'a website'. As a verb 'site' means to build or place something in a particular position: 'The school is sited in the valley'.

Sight

'Sight' refers to the ability to see. The phrase to 'lose your sight' means to become blind. For example, you can say—'The disease has affected his sight'. It also means the act of seeing somebody or something. For instance, 'He was excited at the sight of food'. When soldiers are given orders 'to shoot on sight', they are being asked to shoot as soon as they see somebody. Another meaning is the area or distance within which somebody can be seen: 'There was a dog in sight'. The following are some common expressions formed with 'sight' (1) 'Keep out of sight' (stay where you cannot be seen). (2) 'She never lets her daughter out of her sight' (always keeps her where she can see her). (3) 'Get out of my sight' (Go away).

'Sight' can be used in the countable sense to refer to what you can see. For example, 'He was a sorry sight, soaked to the skin and shivering', or 'The elephant is now a rare sight in the country'. In the plural form, 'sights' refers to interesting places that are often visited by tourists: 'We're going to Cape Coast for the weekend to see the sights'. Other commonly used expressions with 'sight' are explained below. 'At first sight' means when you first begin to consider something: 'At first sight, it may look genuine but always examine the logo beneath the box'. It also means when you see somebody or something for the first time as in the famous expression – 'love at first sight'. Another commonly used expression is 'out of sight, out of mind', which is used to say somebody will quickly be forgotten when they are no longer with you. There is also – 'raise/lower your sights' which means to expect more/less from a situation. Finally, 'a sight for sore eyes' means a person or thing that you are pleased to see or something that is pleasant to look at.

Dictionary Work

Study the meanings of the following words:

1. *allege*
2. *adduce*
3. *aver*
4. *sight-read*
5. *sight unseen*
6. *cynosural*
7. *precinct*
8. *niche*
9. *cantonment*

24

'Disinterested' and 'Uninterested': Revisiting an old dispute

Occasionally, I have been asked about the difference between 'disinterested', and 'uninterested'. These two words, it is argued, should mean the same. One, they have the same root 'interested' which means 'in a position to gain from a situation or be affected by it'. Two, their prefixes – 'dis-' and 'un-' have the same meaning': 'not' or 'the opposite of'. However, the situation is not that straightforward. Surveying dictionaries and books on usage, I have observed that there are a number of scholars who insist on distinguishing the words. How tenable is their position?

Metcalfe and Astle in their book *Correct English* (page 248) argue that 'disinterested' and 'uninterested' do not mean the same. 'Disinterested' means 'neutral, without prejudice, unbiased, impartial, unselfish, not caring one way or the other', while 'uninterested, the direct opposite of interested, is more vehement than disinterested and implies the holding of an impartial view but of a definitely negative view'.

The Merriam-Webster's Dictionary of English Usage (1989), the Collins Cobuild Dictionary, (1998) and the Oxford Advanced Learner's Dictionary (2000) contradict the view of Metcalfe and Astle. The Merriam-Webster's Dictionary of English Usage (1989), for instance, asserts that the alleged confusion between 'disinterested' and 'uninterested' does not exist. It explains that 'disinterested' carries the bulk of use for all meanings, 'uninterested' is much less frequently used. In current use, 'disinterested' has three meanings: an ethical one, 'free from selfish motive or bias'; a simple negative one, 'not interested', and a slightly more emphatic one, 'having lost interest'. Of these, the simple negative is the oldest, the ethical one next, and 'having interest' the most recent.

The Collins Cobuild dictionary also asserts that today, the 'incorrect' use of 'disinterested' is widespread. Around 20% of citations on the British National corpus for 'disinterested' are for this sense.

My view is that 'disinterested' meaning having no personal involvement or receiving no personal advantage, and therefore, free to act fairly should be separated from 'uninterested' which simply means not interested or impassive. This distinction preserves the unique nuance of meaning that 'disinterested' carries[14].

Dictionary Work

Study the meanings of the following words:

1. *inquisitorial*
2. *meddlesome*
3. *prurience*
4. *indifferentism*
5. *impassive*
6. *apathetic*

† See Endnotes at the end of the book.

25

Draught, Draft and Drought

'Draught' and 'Draft', spelt differently, have the same pronunciation /dra:ft/ while 'draught' and 'drought' though remarkably close in spelling (the difference being the contrast between 'a' and 'o') are wide apart in pronunciation and meaning. 'Drought' is pronounced /draut/. Let's examine the relationships between 'draught' and 'draft' on one hand, and 'draught' and 'drought' on the other.

Draught and Draft

To start with, let's examine the basic meanings of 'draught'. 'Draught' refers to a current of air, usually one coming into a room or a vehicle. Example: 'The driver rolled down the window of the car to enjoy the cool draught'. It also refers to a large amount of water or air, which you swallow or breathe in all at one time. Example: 'He gulped the whiskey down in one draught'.

The word 'draught' is also associated with beer. Draught beer is beer that is kept in barrels rather than bottles. Beer that is 'on draught' is kept in and served from a barrel and not from a bottle. Example: 'We have Star on draught'.

'Draughts' refers to a game for two people, each with 12 round pieces on a board of 64 squares. The board on which the game is played is called a draughtsboard.

A draughtsman is someone who is very skilled at drawing; or someone whose job is to prepare very detailed drawings of machinery, equipment, or buildings. It does not refer to a player of the game. There is the combination 'draughts animal' which refers to a horse or donkey used to pull very heavy loads on a farm for example.

A useful adjective formed from 'draught' is 'draughty' which is used to describe a room or a building that has cold air blowing through it.

Now, what's the relationship between 'draught' and 'draft'? While in British English these two words have different meanings, in American English the spelling 'draft' is used for both words. So American English would use 'draft beer', 'beer on draft', 'draftsman', and 'drafty'. Note that in British English 'draft' is used for a preliminary sketch and for the corresponding verb, and also for an order of payment (a bank draft). But 'draught' is used for beer, horses, a current of air, and a game. In American English 'draft' is used in all cases, except the game of draught which is called 'checkers'.

Draught and Drought

As noted above, 'draught' and 'drought' are remarkably close in spelling but wide apart in pronunciation and meaning. It is important to pay some attention to the distinction between these two words because even the most experienced writers sometimes make slips in usage. Indeed, I have come across published material containing the use of 'draught' for 'drought' resulting in serious intelligibility problems.

Remember that 'drought' is pronounced /draut/ and refers to lack or shortage of rainwater, It also means a long period of time during which no rain falls causing extensive damage to crops or preventing their successful growth. Example: 'Ghana suffered from drought in 1983'.

Dictionary Work

Study the meanings of the following words:

1. *flatus*
2. *dram*
3. *sinkage*
4. *blight*
5. *dustbowl*
6. *brief*
7. *design*
8. *aridity*
9. *blueprint*

Flatus: (formal) gas in or from the stomach or intestines, produced by swallowing air or by bacterial fermentation → fletutent/flatulence.

26

Foul and Fowl

A columnist of a Ghanaian weekly, *The Weekend Heritage*, realized to his horror that the heading for his column of that weekend's edition read 'Guinea Foul' instead of 'Guinea Fowl'. Clearly, the 'w' in 'fowl' had been replaced with a 'u'. The columnist subsequently told me that the actual manuscript had had the spelling he intended[15]. But the printer's devil was at his heel, and mischievously rendered the phrase 'Guinea Foul'. The words 'fowl' and 'foul' have the same pronunciation: /faul/; so if you dare the devil a 'fowl' (a bird, especially a chicken) could easily become a 'foul', that is, an action that is against the rules. Let's explore further contexts in which both words are used.

The contexts in which 'fowl' [f-o-w-1] is used are quite limited. It may be used to refer to birds collectively; or specifically to domesticated birds such as, turkey, duck, goose and the guinea fowl. Other uses relate to diseases affecting birds, as in, 'fowl cholera', 'fowl pest' and 'fowl plague'.

'Foul' [f-o-u-1] has a more extensive usage. It may be used as a qualifier to mean offensive to the senses, especially through having a disgusting smell or taste or being unpleasantly soiled. For instance, we can say 'There was a foul smell from the kitchen. Apparently a mouse had died in the washing machine', or 'The water in the tank has become foul'.

You can also use 'foul' to mean unpleasant and not at all enjoyable or successful when making reference to activities or

† See Endnotes at the end of the book.

someone's mood. Examples: 'The news put Kwame in a foul mood', or 'Ama has had a foul day'.

Examples of commonly used expressions formed with 'foul' are – 'foul language', 'foul-mouthed', and 'foul play'. 'Foul language' refers to the use of language that is offensive and contains unacceptable words such as swear words and rude words related to sex and other bodily functions. In short, it refers to the use of coarse or obscene language. Example: 'The author was severely criticised for using foul language in his novel'. A person who uses foul language can be described as 'foul-mouthed'. Example: 'I bumped into a group of foul-mouthed boys at the beach'.

'Foul play' refers to unlawful or dishonest behaviour, especially a violent crime resulting in a person's death. Example: 'There was no evidence of foul play; the man died from natural causes'. The expression is also used in sports to refer to unfair play; that is, when players do something that is not allowed by the rules. Example: 'The coach advised his players to avoid foul play'.

There are other useful expressions like 'by fair or foul means', 'fall foul of', and 'foul up'. 'By fair or foul means' is used to show you are prepared to use any means at all in order to get what you want and you do not care if your behaviour is dishonest and unfair. Example: 'He wants to be chairman by fair or foul means'.

'Fall foul of means to do something which makes someone angry with you, or which breaks a rule with the result that you are punished. You can also say 'to run foul of'. Example: 'If Kwesi falls/runs foul of the authorities he will lose his job'.

Finally, if you 'foul up' something such as a plan, you spoil it by doing something wrong or stupid. Example: 'The manager fouled up our plans with his misguided utterances'.

Dictionary Work

Study the meanings of the following words:

1. squalor
2.insalubrity
3. fustiness
4. fledgeling
5. carrion crow
6. adjutant bird

27

Flash and Flush

As we have observed in a previous unit, some individuals tend to use the vowel /a/ in place of /æ/ and / ʌ /as found in the words: man /æ/, back /æ/, must / m ʌ st / and buck / b ʌ k /. The words 'flash' and 'flush' fall into the same category. Note that 'flash' is pronounced /flæʃ/ while 'flush' is pronounced /flʌʃ /.

Flash

A flash of light is a very bright light which comes suddenly and disappears immediately, like lightning in a storm. Example: 'There was a flash of light in the darkness'. If a light flashes or if you flash a light, it shines with a very bright light, especially as quick, regular flashes of light. Example: 'He flashed his headlights at us'. In American English, a flash is also the same as a torch.

Drawing from the metaphor of light, 'flash' is used idiomatically in many contexts to depict suddenness, speed, and shortness. A few examples are provided below: 'A white object flashed past the moving train.' (the object moved very fast); 'John was out of the room in a flash.' (the incident was immediate, sudden, and short); 'It flashed through her mind that she might never see him again.' (the thought or the image appeared suddenly and then immediately disappeared).

Other uses related to rapidity or suddenness of occurrence are as follows: A flash of a particular emotion or experience is something that you experience suddenly and unexpectedly.

Example: 'John had a flash of anger at being taken for granted'. If someone's eyes flash, they express a sudden strong emotion, especially anger. Example: 'Kofi's eyes flashed when he was told to leave the conference'. If you flash a look or a smile at someone, you look at them suddenly in the way mentioned. Example: 'She flashed a loving smile at her daughter'. If you flash something, you show it to people quickly and then put it away again. Example: 'She flashed her identification card at the guards'. If you flash information or news to a particular place, you send it quickly by computer, satellite, telex, etc. Example: 'The news had been flashed to all the neighbouring countries'.

Apart from the meanings illustrated above, there are other uses worthy of note: Something that has a flash of a particular colour on it has a small patch of bright colour on it. Example: 'Ama's blue dress had a flash of red on the sleeves'. Something that looks flash looks expensive, fashionable, and new. This use is informal. Example: 'Kwame's new car looks really flash'. A common qualifier is 'flashy', which is used in the sense—smart, bright, and expensive that you find it unpleasant and perhaps vulgar. Example: 'a flashy car'. If you describe an achievement or success as a flash in the pan, you mean that it is not likely to be repeated and is not an indication of future achievement or successes. Example: 'The manager's initial enthusiasm seems to have been a flash in the pan'.

A flash burn is a burn that you get if you are near an extremely bright, hot place, for example, a flash caused by an exploding bomb. (Compare with 'hot flush' below). A flashpoint is the moment at which emotional or political conflict reaches a climax and becomes violent. Example: 'The crisis in Iraq has reached a flashpoint'. The word may also be used to refer to a place which people think is dangerous because political trouble may start there and then spread to other towns or countries. Example: 'The town is another very possible flashpoint because of the chieftaincy dispute'.

Flush

The opening definition for 'flush' in the numerous dictionaries I have surveyed is – 'to become red in the face or blush'; a phenomenon probably unfamiliar to black Africans. Your face goes red because you feel hot or unwell or because you are embarrassed. Occasionally, I have heard some people joke about dark-skinned persons 'blushing'. Conceivably the context in which you may have to use 'flush' in the sense just explained may be limited depending on the colour of your skin; nonetheless, there are other uses which should be of benefit to you. These are explained below.

Another basic meaning of 'flush' relates to washing something out by a sudden flow of water. For example, when you flush a toilet or when it flushes, the handle is pressed or pulled and the toilet bowl is emptied of its waste matter, after which the water refills. You can also flush somebody or something out, meaning to force that person or (it could be) an animal to vacate their hiding place. An example sentence is – 'The police flushed the armed robbers out of their den'. In many cities, towns and villages in Africa it is common to see children and young men using smoke, as a hunting method, to flush out rodents from their holes.

Furthermore, 'flush' can be used to signify a sudden or intense feeling of excitement or pleasure about something. Example: 'When the teacher broke the news of Mary's son's failure in the entrance examination to her a flush of anger tore through her body'. 'Flush can also be used to mean a large amount of something that appears suddenly or quickly'. Example: 'There is always a flush of snails when the rains come'.

Finally, 'hot flush' refers to a sudden hot feeling in the skin which women often experience at the time of their menopause. It is used mainly in British English.

Dictionary Work

Study the meanings of the following words:

1. *flash in the pan*
2. *flash flood*
3. *flash house*
4. *flushed with success*
5. *in the first flush of*

28

Guard and Guide

One day I went to a Communication Centre whose a caption caught my eye—'Guardlines'. Clearly, what was intended was–'Guidelines'. Let's examine the differences between 'guard' and 'guide' so we don't get confused when using them.

Guard

'To guard' is to protect a person, place, or valuable object by staying near them. For example: 'The policeman guards the house when the family is on holiday'. The phrasal verb 'to guard against' means to try to prevent something from happening by being careful. Example: 'Drivers must guard against accidents always'.

As a noun a 'guard' refers to someone whose job is to protect a place, person, or object from attack or from thieves. Example: 'The guard stopped the thieves from breaking into the house'. Below are some expressions formed with the word 'guard'.

'Be under guard' is to be under the protection of a group of people with weapons. Example: 'The chairman is under guard 24 hours a day'. 'To throw somebody off guard' is to surprise the person by doing or saying something that they are not ready to deal with. Example: 'His question threw the speaker off guard'. You can also use the expressions, 'catch somebody off guard' and 'take somebody off guard'.

'To be on your guard' means to pay careful attention to what is happening so that you avoid being tricked or getting into danger. Example: 'You have to be on your guard when you visit crowded places'. The opposite of the expression above is 'to lower your guard' or 'to let your guard down' which means to stop being careful.

The qualifier 'guarded' as used for statements and remarks means the speaker deliberately withholds information about his or her thoughts or feelings. Example: 'The politician made a guarded appeal to the angry crowd'.

Guide

'To guide' is to show someone the right way to do something, especially something difficult or complicated. Example: 'We need an expert to guide us to operate the machine'. 'Guide' can also be used to mean to strongly influence someone's behaviour. Example: 'His wife guides him in all his actions'.

'A guide' is a person who shows someone the way to a place, especially someone whose job is to show a place to tourists. Example: 'The tour guide took us through the damp rooms of the old castle'. 'A guide' also refers to someone who advises people and influences the way they live.

A book that provides information on a particular subject or explains how to do something may be referred to as a 'guide'. This is synonymous with handbook. Take note of 'guidebook' which refers to a special book about a city providing information about the place and its history.

Take note of the following words: 'guided missile', 'guide dog', 'guided tour', and 'guidelines' which was mentioned in the introductory paragraph. The word 'guidelines' refers to official instructions about the best way to do something, especially something that could be difficult or dangerous. If you say 'guardlines' you may be referring to a line of protection!

Dictionary Work

Study the meanings of the following words:

1. *guardrail*
2. *guardroom*
3. *guardsman*
4. *prototype*
5. *itinerary*
6. *circumnavigation*

29

Heal Your Heels

'Heal' and 'Heels' have the same pronunciation – /hi:l/, but evidently their spelling is different which could be a potential source of confusion. 'Heal' means to make whole, sound, or well, bring back to health or become healthy and normal again. Remember Luke 4:23 – 'Physician, heal thyself'. This biblical proverb means that people should take care of their own defects not just correct the fault of others. Your 'heel' is the back part of your foot, just below your ankle. It also refers to the raised part of your shoe at the back. The heel of your hand is the rounded pad at the bottom of your palm. Let's take a closer look at the meanings of each word.

Heal

The word 'heal' is used in a medical sense to mean cure someone who is ill or to restore a cut, broken bone, or other injury to a healthy and normal state. Examples: (a) 'His broken arm will heal in no time', (b) 'The medicine will heal the cut eventually'. To heal someone who has an illness means to make them recover. Example: 'The herbalist healed the patient in no time'. A healer is a person who heals people. If you heal something, you restore it to its former state after it has been damaged. Example: 'The war has left deep wounds that only time may heal'.

Note the phrasal verb – 'heal over' which has the following meanings: (a) If a wound or an area of broken skin heals over, new skin grows over it and it becomes healthy again, (b) If an argument heals over or is healed over, it is forgotten. In a figurative sense, 'heal' means to free from anything bad, save or cleanse.

The form 'healing' may be used as a qualifier to mean something that heals or cures, as in 'a healing salve'. It could also be used to mean growing sound or well as in 'the healing process'.

Heels

There are a number of expressions formed with 'heels'. These include: click your heels, dig your heels in, drag your heels, follow hard on the heels of, tread hard on somebody's heels, cool your heels, and head over heels. Let's examine them.

To click your heels means to make a sharp sound with the heels of your shoes, especially by knocking them together as part of a military salute. Example: 'The soldier walked briskly to the room and clicked his heels'. Now, if you dig your heels in, you refuse to do something such as change your opinions or plans, especially when someone is trying very hard to make you do so. Example: 'The director digs his heels in whenever the staff are too persistent in their demands'. You can also drag your heels meaning you do something unwillingly and with deliberate slowness. Example: 'I don't understand why the students have not come to this reconciliatory meeting; they're certainly dragging their heels'.

If one event or situation follows hard on the heels of another, it happens very quickly or immediately after it. Example: 'A cyclone followed immediately on the heels of the earthquake'.

To tread hard on somebody's heels or to be hot on their heels means to follow them very close behind. Example: 'The beggars were treading hard on the manager's heels, asking for money'.

If you are cooling your heels or kicking your heels, someone is deliberately keeping you waiting, so that you get bored or impatient. Example: 'The lady was cooling her heels in the secretary's office'. To be head over heels in love with someone means you are very much in love. Example: 'The young man is head over heels in love with the middle aged spinster'.

This unit's heading 'Heal your heels' captures the difference in meaning between the two words: 'heal' meaning cure and 'heels' the back part of your feet, may be you have developed blisters on them; so cure your heels.

Dictionary Work

Study the meanings of the following words:

1. *cicatrize*
2. *rejuvenate*
3. *cooperative*
4. *nadir*
5. *epilogue*
6. *topsy-turvy*

30

Lamp and Lump

As is generally known, a lamp is a device which produces light by burning oil (remember the biblical story of the Ten Virgins and the lamp oil?) or gas or by using electricity. Very early in our lives, most of us whether village-bred, town-bred, or city-bred must have encountered this word and the device it refers to one way or another. In our part of the world, access to electricity is limited, and electricity power generation itself is so unreliable that many people resort to the use of candles and oil or gas powered lamps. Later in life you come across 'lump' (that is spelt with a 'u') used in reference to a growth on someone's body, or in reference to detecting signs of breast cancer. As we have observed in previous units, many Ghanaian speakers of English tend to use the vowel sound /a/ for the vowels /æ/ and /ʌ/ in monosyllabic words such as 'back/buck' and 'flash/ flush'. 'Lamp' and 'lump' fall into the same category. Let's consider meaning differences between the two and contexts in which they are used.

Lamp

As explained above, a lamp is a device for producing light. Words that are associated with it are – 'lamplight', 'lamplit', 'lamppost', and 'lampshade'. Lamplight is the light produced by a lamp; while the derivative 'lamplit' refers to the situation where something can be seen because there is light from a lamp. 'Lamppost' is a tall thin support for a lamp which lights a street or other public area while 'lampshade' refers to a cover placed over a lamp in order to reduce or direct its light. So when you use the spelling

'1-a-m-p', note that you are referring to the contexts described above.

Lump

Let's now turn our attention to 'lump'. A lump is a piece of a solid substance, of any shape or size. Example: 'Lumps of meat'. A lump on or in someone's body is a small, hard piece of flesh that is formed as a result of an injury or an illness. Example: 'Women have to examine their breasts for lumps'. Something that is lumpy contains lumps or is covered with lumps. Example: 'The fufu is lumpy'.

Lump is also used to refer to an amount of something, especially money that you use, give, or receive as one large amount on a single occasion rather than as smaller amounts on several separate occasions. Therefore, a 'lump sum' refers to an amount of money that is paid as a large amount on a single occasion rather than as smaller amounts on several separate occasions. Example: 'These days shop owners prefer lump sum payments to payments by instalments', or 'The workers insisted that their salary arrears be paid in a lump sum'.

Further uses of lump are as follows: If you say that someone has a lump in their throat, you mean that they have a tight feeling in their throat because of a strong emotion such as sorrow or gratitude. Example: 'The sight of the gory accident brought a lump to his throat'. If you say that someone will lump it or will have to lump it, you mean that they must accept a situation or decision whether they like it or not. Example: 'The Board of Directors has taken a decision; therefore, if the accountant doesn't like it, he can lump it'. If you lump different people or things together, you consider or treat them in the same way or combine them into one large group, especially without thinking or caring about them very much. Example: 'All the detainees were lumped together in one room in spite of their sex'.

Dictionary Work

Study the meanings of the following words:

1. *illuminant*
2. *corpse candle*
3. *flambeau*
4. *roll into one*
5. *muddle*
6. *confound*

31

Loose and Lose

Some people tend to confuse the word 'loose' with 'lose' and vice versa. We shall examine the contexts of use of both words. Loose /lu:s/ can be used as an adjective, verb and noun. The basic meaning of this word is 'not firmly fixed where it should be'; or 'able to become separated from something'. For example, you can say—'a loose button or tooth'. Lose /lu:z/ is a verb; and it means 'to be unable to find something or somebody' or 'to have something or somebody taken away from you by accident, old age, death, etc. For instance, 'If a child keeps playing with your keys, you may lose them', or 'The injury from the car crash is so severe she may lose a leg'.

Let's examine further contexts in which 'lose' and 'loose' occur.

Lose

'Lose' can be used to mean 'to escape from something' as in – 'We managed to lose our pursuers in the darkness'. Some idiomatic expressions formed with 'lose' are listed below: (1) 'Lose out on something' (not get something you wanted or feel you should have'. For example, you can say – 'While the stores make big profits, it's the customer who loses out'. (2) 'Lose yourself in something' (to become so interested in something that it takes all your attention). (3) 'Lose out to somebody or something' (not get business etc. that you expected or used to get because somebody or something else has taken it) as in 'Small businesses are losing out to the large chains'.

Loose

'Loose' can be used to refer to (1) clothes when you mean they don't fit closely: 'a loose jacket'; (2) not tightly packed together; not solid or hard: 'loose soil'; (3) not strictly organised or controlled: 'a loose alliance'; (4) not very careful: 'loose thinking'; (5) having or involving an attitude to sexual relationships that people consider to be immoral: 'a young man of loose morals'.

Remember that the word with a double 'o' 'loose' is pronounced /lu:s/ note the 's' sound at the end of the word; while the word with a single 'o' 'lose' is pronounced /lu:z/ with a 'z' sound at the end of it. The primary distinction in meaning is that 'loose' has to do with 'not firmly fixed' while 'lose' concerns 'unable to find something' or 'have something taken away from you'. Thus whenever you write any of these words do a simple meaning check. Another strategy is to consider whether you are using the word as a verb, adjective or noun. You would have noticed that while 'lose' is mainly used as a verb 'loose' can occur as a verb, noun and adjective. So when you write 'lose change' you should note that it is wrong and that the correct form is 'loose change'. 'Lose' cannot occur as a qualifier.

Dictionary Work

Study the meanings of the following words:

1. lossen your tongue
2. be at a loose end
3. on the loose
4. loose change
5. loose cannon
6. lose your head
7. lose the plot
8. lose your rag
9. lose sleep over/about something lose heart

32

Portable and Potable

There is a difference between 'portable' and 'potable'. Apart from the difference in spelling there is a difference in pronunciation and meaning. But we notice that most people tend to use 'portable' when what they actually mean is 'potable'. 'Portable' is also used in contexts that are not easy to defend or explain. So we shall examine the differences between the two words and then take a closer look at the uses of 'portable' in the Ghanaian context.

'Portable' is pronounced /pɔ:təbəl/ while 'potable' is pronounced /pəutəbəl/. The confusion probably stems from the pronunciation of 'pot' and 'port' in Ghanaian contexts. Ghanaians don't really make a distinction between 'port' /pɔ:t/ (the place where ships load and unload goods, e.g., The Tema Port), and 'pot' /pɒt/ (a container used for cooking things in). So when we see the words 'portable' and 'potable' why bother about checking their pronunciations? But pronunciation does really matter here. Let's check the meaning of the two words.

Potable

'Potable' on the other hand means 'safe or suitable to drink'. So we can say, 'There is no supply of potable water'. If we had used 'portable' instead of 'potable' the above sentence would read close to 'We do not have water that is movable'. So let's remember that when talking about water that is safe or drinkable, the word we should use is 'potable', spelt without an 'r', and pronounced /pəutəbəl/.

Portable

'Portable', as an adjective, refers to having the quality of being easily carried or moved about especially because the thing is of a lighter and smaller version than usual. So we can talk of 'a portable television'. As a noun, it refers to a version of something such as a small lightweight television or computer that can be easily carried. For example, we can say, 'We bought a black portable'. in reference to the portable item.

Let us take a closer look at the use of 'portable' in the Ghanaian context. People tend to use 'portable' to qualify houses, women and cars. For instance, we hear expressions such as 'a portable house', 'the woman is portable', and 'a portable car'. Based on the definition of 'portable' what we are saying in effect is that the entities so described can be easily carried or moved about. In North American English the expression 'a portable house' refers to a small transportable building used as a classroom. Unfortunately, we don't have such a facility in Ghana. The closest we have is what we popularly refer to as 'containers'. They are indeed containers but probably after transforming them into shops and mini-restaurants we can call them 'portable houses'?

As regards the expression 'the woman is portable', what we probably mean is small and attractive. Let's remember that women are neither gadgets nor pieces of machinery. So let's use alternative expressions like, 'cute' or 'petite', or some other more appropriate descriptive word or phrase. I don't quite understand the reference to cars as 'portable'. Probably those in the car towing business may appreciate its import. Does the reference mean small and therefore easy to be carried away or moved about? Avoid describing cars as portable since they are not made to be carried about.

Dictionary Work

Look up the meanings and the parts of speech of the following words:

1. *potability*
2. *potableness*
3. *nonpotable*
4. *portability*
5. *portableness*
6. *portably*

33

Reign and Rein

'Reign' and 'rein' have the same pronunciation - /rein/ with different meanings[16]. Some writers misinterpret them and use 'reign' in contexts where 'rein' should have been used. Take note of the meanings of both words and the contexts in which they are used. Whenever you are in doubt don't hesitate, go for a dictionary.

Reign

Used as noun, 'reign' refers to the period of time during which someone is king or queen. It also refers to a period during which something is the most powerful or most important feature of a place. Examples: (1) 'The reign of King Tackie Tawiah I' (2) 'The reign of violence in civil wars...'.

As a verb, 'reign' means to be the king or queen. Example: 'King Opoku Ware II reigned in the 20th century'. It also means to be the most important feature of a place at a particular time. Example: 'During the civil war anarchy reigned for many years'.

The phrase 'the reigning champion' refers to the most recent winner of a competition. Example: 'The reigning featherweight champion was on TV'.

Rein

'Rein' in its literal sense refers to a long narrow band of leather that is fastened around a horse's head in order to control it. Quite a number of idiomatic expressions are derived from this meaning.

---

† See Endnotes at the end of the book.

'To give full/free rein to' means to allow an emotion or feeling to be expressed freely. Example: 'Mr. Chairman, kindly allow members to give free rein to their feelings so we can have fruitful discussions'.

'To give somebody (a) free rein' is to give the person complete freedom to decide how they are going to do a particular task. Examples: (1) 'The director has given the secretary free rein to handle his visitors'. (2) 'The police boss gave his men free rein to deal with the armed robbers'.

When you keep a tight rein on somebody or something, you control the person or thing firmly or strictly. Examples: (1) 'The housemaster keeps a tight rein on the students'. (2) 'We will have to keep a tight rein on expenditure because of the oil crisis'.

'To take or hand over the reins' is to take or give someone control over an organisation or country. Examples: (1) 'The rebels want to take over the reins of government'. (2) 'It became clear after the elections that the incumbent President was unwilling to hand over the reins of government even though he had completed his term of office'.

Dictionary Work

Study the meanings of the following words:

1. *regency*
2. *monocracy*
3. *oligarchy*
4. *noose*
5. *shackle*
6. *fetter*

34

Resort and Result

'Resort' is pronounced /rɪzɔ:t/ while 'result' is pronounced /rɪzʌlt/. Take note of the difference between their last syllables /zɔ:t/ for 'resort' and /zʌlt/ for 'result'. Now let's consider their meanings.

Resort

As a noun, 'resort' refers to a place where people often go for holidays. Example: 'a seaside resort', 'a beach resort'. It is also used to refer to a place that a person or a particular group of people often visits. Example: 'This internet café is a favourite resort of businessmen'.

The expressions 'as a last resort' and 'in the last resort' are used to say what you will do if everything else fails. Example: 'All the elders of the church refused to help us. As a last resort we decided to talk to the chairman of the Welfare Committee'. There is also the expression 'of last resort' which is used when you have tried a lot of other things and they have all failed. Example: 'a weapon of last resort'.

'Resort to' means to use something or do something that is bad, in order to succeed or deal with a problem. Example: 'When his mother refused to give him extra pocket money, Kwame resorted to stealing'. Additionally, we have the expression 'have to resort to' which means to do something bad or extreme because you cannot think of any other solution. Example: 'If he fails to deliver our goods, it may be necessary to have to resort to force'.

Result

As a verb, 'result' means to happen or exist because of something. We have the combination 'result from'. Example: 'His problems result from his careless attitude to life'. There is also 'result in', which means to make something happen. It is synonymous with 'cause'. Example: The accident resulted in the death of many people.

As a noun, 'result' refers to something that happens or exists because of something that happened before. We normally have the combination 'result of' Examples: 'The result of laziness is failure' and 'His illness is the result of excessive smoking'.

A common expression is 'as a result of' which means because of something that has happened. Example: 'As a result of the violence, all children have been asked to stay at home'.

Another useful expression is 'with the result that'. Example: 'John wasn't at the meeting, with the result that he missed a critical opportunity'. There is also 'be a direct result (of)' which means 'caused by one thing only'. Example: 'His vigour is a direct result of his healthy lifestyle'.

Some people wonder whether it is right to say, 'end result'. The answer is 'yes', and the expression means 'the result at the end of a long process'. Similar expressions are 'final result' and 'net result'. Example: 'The end result of these marketing reforms is that the company will maximise profit'.

'Result' or 'results' is used in several other contexts – sports, elections, scientific tests, examination and business.

Dictionary Work

Study the meanings of the following words:

1. *corradiation*
2. *cynosure*
3. *recourse*
4. *dénouement*
5. *repercussion*
6. *derivation*

35

Round and Around

'Round' and 'Around' may be regarded, in a jocular fashion, as linguistic siblings since they are similar in most respects except one—the 'a' in the spelling of 'around'. Indeed, they are interchangeable in many contexts. However, there are certain contexts where one is generally preferred to the other. We shall examine some of these contexts.

Round

First, let's consider the basic meaning of 'round'. 'Round' is used to refer to something that is shaped like a ball or a circle. That is the kind of meaning in expressions like – 'The earth is round', and 'The man has a round face'. The word 'round' also means curved in shape, like the letter 'c'. For example, one can say – 'In the distance, we could see the clear round bulge of the man's stomach'.

Let's also look at other meanings of 'round'. 'Round' is used to describe the eyes of people if they are open very wide, usually because they are excited or surprised as in 'John's eyes were round with excitement'. It may also be used to refer to a number or a figure to show that it is an easy number to remember because it is a whole number, probably ending with 'O'. Example: 'That's a nice round figure'.

'Round' may be combined with a preposition to yield a variety of meanings. Here are a few examples. 'Round on' (make a sudden verbal attack on or unexpected retort).

Example: 'She rounded on John angrily'. 'Round something out' (make something more complete). Example: 'His father insisted he went to university to round out his education'. 'Round someone or something up' (drive or collect a number of people or animals together for a particular purpose). Example: 'The police rounded up the armed robbers'. In this usage, it also simply means 'arrest a number of people'.

Having looked at contexts in which 'round' is not interchangeable with 'around', let's examine contexts where 'around', is solely used.

Around

'Around' is used to mean someone or something is present or available. Examples: 'He checked the rooms to see who was around', or 'It's a familiar old gadget which has been around for hundreds of years'. Additionally, if someone 'has been around', he or she has had a lot of experience of different people, places, life-styles, and situations. Examples: 'I've been around and I know how to handle people like him'. Note, however, that this usage is considered informal.

We now turn our attention to contexts where 'round' and 'around' are interchangeable.

You use 'round' or 'around' to indicate that something is positioned or arranged on all the sides of someone or something, or that it forms a circle on the outside of them. Example: 'We were sitting round/around a table eating'. You may also use 'round/ around' to indicate that something is situated on the other side of something. Examples: 'The dustbins are round/ around the back of the house', and 'There are a couple of stops just around/round the corner'.

Dictionary Work

Study the following idioms formed with 'round' and 'around':

1. *a clip round the ear*
2. *be like a millstone around/roundyour neck*
3. *be/go round the twist*
4. *drive/send somebody round the bend*
5. *get your mind round something*
6. *go all round the houses*
7. *go/run round in circles*
8. *have something/somebody hanging round your neck*
9. *run rings round*
10. *run round like a headless chicken*
11. *word gets around/round*
12. *beat around the bush*
13. *can't get your head around*
14. *fray around at the edges*
15. *know your way around*
16. *make the world go around/round*
17. *pass the hat around/round*
18. *sit around on your backside*
19. *throw your weight around/about*
20. *twist somebody around/round your little finger*
21. *work your way around/round to something*

36

Scrap and Scrape

There are many differences between 'scrap' and 'scrape'. 'Scrap' is pronounced /skræp/ and 'scrape' is pronounced /skreip/. Let's examine some of the meaning differences between the two words.

Scrap

'Scarp' as a noun refers to a small piece of something, especially paper or fabric. For example, 'He scribbled his phone number on a scrap of paper'. In figurative terms, it can used in the sense – 'scraps of news or information'. There is also the meaning 'a small amount of something', as in 'It won't make a scrap of difference'; or 'There's not a scrap of evidence to support his claim'. The plural form 'scraps' refers to food left after a meal: 'Give the scraps to the dog'. In the uncountable sense, the word 'scrap' refers to things that are not wanted or cannot be used for their original purpose but which have some value for the material they are made of: 'We sold the car for scrap' (so that any good parts can be used again). For example, 'scrap metal' or 'a scrap dealer'.

As a verb, 'scrap' means 'to cancel or get rid of something that is not longer practical or useful'; 'The district assembly was forced to scrap plans for a new school building'.

Scrape

'Scrape' means to remove something from a surface by moving something hard like a knife across it: 'She scraped the mud off her shoes'. It also means to rub something accidentally so that it gets damaged or hurt: 'I scraped the side of my car on the wall'. or 'She fell and scraped her knee'. Another meaning of 'scrape' is to make an unpleasant noise by rubbing against a hard surface: 'I could hear his pen scraping across the paper'. or 'Don't scrape your chairs on the floor'. 'Scrape' also means manage to win or to get something with difficulty: 'The team scraped a narrow victory last year'. or 'They scraped a living by selling apples on the streets'. When you scrape your hair back, you pull your hair tightly back away from your face: 'Her hair was scraped back from her face in a ponytail'.

Here are some examples of idiomatic expressions formed with 'scrape': (1) 'scrape (the bottom of) the barrel' means to have to use whatever things or people you can get because there is not much choice available. (2) 'scrape by (on something)': to manage to live on the money you have, but with difficulty: 'I can just scrape by on what my parents give me'. (3) 'scrape in or scrape into something': to manage to get a job, a position, or a place but with difficulty. For example, we can say 'Our team just scraped into the semi-finals'. (4) 'Scrape through or scrape through something'; to succeed in doing something with difficulty, especially in passing an exam. For example, 'I might scrape through the exam if I'm lucky'.

As a noun, 'scrape' refers to the action or unpleasant sound of one thing rubbing roughly against another: 'the scrape of iron on stone'. It also refers to an injury or mark caused by rubbing against something rough: 'She emerged from the overturned car with only a few scrapes and bruises'.

Dictionary Work

Study the meanings of the following words:

1. smithereens	*4. stridulate*
2. desuetude	*5. grate*
3. superannuation	*6. gravel*

37

Sever and Severe

I believe most people have found themselves in situations where on coming across the word 'sever' have paused to think of its close resemblance to 'severe'. Indeed, I have heard people pronounce, 'sever' as if it were 'severe'. Let's examine the pronunciations and uses of both words.

Sever

'Sever' is pronounced /sevə/ and grammatically it is a verb. Its derivatives are—severs, severing, severed.

'To sever something' means to cut right through it so that one part is completely separated from the rest of it. Example: 'The car severed the dog's head from its body'.

'Sever' is also used to mean break off as in relationships. So if you sever a relationship or connection that you have with someone, you end it suddenly, completely, and for ever. Example: 'John had to sever all ties with his parents'.

Severe

'Severe' is pronounced / si'vlə /. Grammatically, it is used mainly as a qualifier, that is, an adjective or an adverb. There is also the noun form 'severity'.

'Severe' is used of something bad or undesirable that is very great in degree. Example: 'There is a severe shortage of food in Accra'.

If you describe someone as severe, you mean the person treats people harshly and is unwilling to forgive their mistakes or weakness. Example: 'The teacher was severe with his students'.

Someone who is severe is stern, unfriendly, and lacking in kindness or humour. Example: 'He spoke to his wife in a severe voice'.

'Severe' can also be used to describe a style of appearance that is plain and simple, with little or no decoration. In this sense, it is synonymous with austere. Example: 'On auction was a picture of a man in severe traditional battle costume'.

The forms 'severely' (adverb) and 'severity' (noun) may also be used. Examples: 'They were severely punished'; or 'The people complained about the severity of the prison sentences'.

Dictionary Work

Study the meanings of the following words:

1. *disjoin*
2. *diverge*
3. *uncouple*
4. *anstere*
5. *puritanial*
6. *hypercritical*

38

Stake and Steak

'Stake' and 'steak' have the same pronunciation – /steik/ but are spelt differently, and have different meanings. Let's examine the different meanings.

Steak

'Steak' simply refers to good quality beef, or a large thick piece of any good quality red meat. For example, you can say, 'I enjoy hot pepper steak'. 'Steak' also refers to a large thick piece of fish.

Some Ghanaian restaurants serve 'steak'. In some countries you can find restaurants that mainly serve 'steak'. They are called 'steakhouses', pronounced /steikhauziz/. Of course, the singular form is 'steakhouse' /steikhaus/.

Stake

'Stake' has more meanings than 'steak'. As a noun it may be used to refer to a pointed piece of wood or metal that is pushed into the ground to hold a rope or mark a particular place. Historically, it also refers to a post to which a person was tied to be killed by being burnt. A common expression in this regard is: 'burn somebody at the stake'.

If something that you value very much is at stake, you will lose it if a plan or action is not successful. For example: 'John's job was at stake after he failed to impress the Board of Directors of the company'.

'To have a stake in' is to have an important part or share in a business or plan so that you will gain if it succeeds. For example: 'All workers have a stake in their company's business'.

In this same meaning area, if someone stakes a business or company they support it by supplying it with money or other financial help. For example: 'The Government stakes ¢10 million a month in the company'.

Another useful expression formed with 'stake' is 'go to the stake for/over something', which means to take great risks to protect or defend an idea or belief. For example: 'He's prepared to go to the stake for his political beliefs'.

'Stakes' refer to money that people risk on the result of a game or a race, all of which is taken by the winner. For example: 'The stakes are high in this game'.

A related expression is – 'to play for high stakes' which refers to (1) risking a lot of money in a game, as in 'We're playing for high stakes in this game', and (2) being in a situation where you gain or lose a lot.

There are a few useful expressions formed with 'stake' as a verb. 'To stake' is to risk money on a race or competition For example: 'He risked his whole fortune on one card game'. Another meaning is to risk losing something that is valuable or important to you, if a plan or action is not successful. For example: 'The fertile part of the land was staked off'.

'To stake (out) a claim' is to say publicly that you think you have a right to have or own something. For example: 'The man staked his claim to the farm when he discovered his family heirloom on it'.

A word that has become vogue in Ghana is 'stakeholder'. It is used to mean anyone who has an interest in or tends to benefit from an institution, or organization, or from a process. A stakeholder also means someone chosen to hold the money that is risked by people on a race or a competition, and to give all of it to the winner, or someone, normally a lawyer, who takes charge of property during a quarrel or a sale.

Dictionary Work

Study the meanings of the following words:

1. *wager*
2. *imperil*
3. *jeopardize*
4. *venture*
5. *spurn the odds*
6. *tempt providence*

39

Straight and Strait

'Straight' and 'strait' have the same pronunciation: /streit/. So sometimes people confuse the two. To avoid this, you have to take particular note of their spelling and their meaning differences.

Straight

Though the word 'straight' occurs frequently in everyday usage, I would like us to review some of its meanings. 'Straight' is used to refer to something that goes in one direction and does not bend or curve. We typically talk of 'straight lines' and 'straight roads'. When giving someone directions it is not uncommon to say: 'Go straight till you get to the roundabout'.

Let's consider other meanings of 'straight'. 'Straight' is used to mean immediately or without delay. Example: 'We can meet straight after the party'. In this usage the following words may be used after straight – 'to', 'down', and 'back'.

Here are a few examples: (1) 'When the meeting started the Chairman didn't waste time at all, he got straight down to business'. (2) 'Come straight back home after the beach party'. (3) He went straight to the bedroom.

If you are straight with someone it means you are honest and truthful. Example: 'He gave the policeman straight answers'. Associated expressions are – 'straight talk', 'straight honesty'.

We use the expression 'get this straight' or 'get it straight' to indicate you want to understand the true facts about a situation.

Example: 'Let me get this straight: the secretary signed the letter and collected the goods from the warehouse'?

'To keep a straight face' is to hold back from laughing. Example: 'The students kept a straight face when the lecturer fell off his bicycle'. 'Straight' can also be used in reference to alcoholic drinks. Alcoholic drinks that are straight have no water or ice or any other liquid added. Example: 'I like my gin straight'. This is synonymous with 'neat': 'He likes his whisky neat'.

Strait

'Strait' is often used in the plural. It refers to a narrow passage of water between two areas of land, usually connecting two seas. Example: 'The Strait of Gibraltar'.

'Straits' also means difficulty or hardship. A common expression is – 'be in dire straits', which means to be in a difficult situation, especially a financial one that could have very bad or dangerous results. Example: 'The Company is in dire straits as a result of the incompetence of the Board of Directors'.

Note that 'straitjacket' is also spelt 'straightjacket'. This word means (a) a special piece of clothing that is used to control the movement of someone who is mentally ill and violent and (b) a law or set of ideas that puts unfair limits on someone; or anything that prevents freedom of development or expression.

Dictionary Work

Study the meanings of the following words:

1. *rectilinear*
2. *inflexible*
3. *unfrizzed*
4. *scrupulous*
5. *squeamish*
6. *incorruptible*

40

Laughing Stock or Stalk?

Sometimes I encounter the word 'stalk' used in place of 'stock' in the expression 'laughing stock'. The mistake is probably due to the perceived closeness in pronunciation between the two words: Stock /stɒk/ Stalk / stɔk/. Note that the correct word is 'stock'. 'Laughing stock' may be used to refer to a person who seems stupid or ridiculous in an attempt to be serious or important and not succeeding. Let's examine the meanings and contexts of use of 'stalk' and 'stock'.

Stalk

As a noun, 'stalk' refers to the main stem of a plant, or the narrow stem that joins leaves, flowers or fruit to the main stem of a plant. It also refers to a narrow structure that supports a part of the body in some animals. Beyond these basic meanings, 'stalk' in the humorous expression 'eyes out on stalks' means your eyes are wide open with surprise. For example: 'Her eyes were out on stalks when she saw her husband dancing enthusiastically with the teenager'.

The phrase 'stalking horse' is used to describe someone who has no chance of winning a position but is used by a group of politicians to compete for that position in order to divide the opposition or to take attention away from another person who they really want to win. The 2000 general elections in Ghana provided a classic example. The NDC suffered collateral damage as a result of the breakaway National Reform Party (NRP) whose candidates constituted 'stalking horses', as it were, in certain constituencies considered to be 'safe' for the NDC. It was clear that the NRP candidates were not going to win. The final outcome proved the situation that the NRP candidates took away crucial votes from the NDC paving the way for the NPP.

The verb 'to stalk' means to follow an animal or person as closely as possible without being seen or heard, usually in order to catch or kill them: 'The policemen stalked the criminals for several days'. The word 'stalk' also means to illegally follow and watch someone, usually a woman, over a period of time: 'Ama remembered the days when her boyfriend stalked her all over the market'. A 'stalker' is a person who illegally follows and watches someone over a period of time.

Stock

'Stock' means a supply of something for use or sale; or the total number of goods or the amount of a particular type of goods available in a shop. In business contexts, 'stock' is used in combination with several words as in: stockholder, stockbroker, stock control, stock market etc. Take note of the expressions—'put stock in something' and 'take stock of something'.

'Put stock in something' means to have a high opinion of something that someone says or does. Example: 'Kofi has never been on time, so I don't put much stock in his appointments anymore'. 'To take stock of something' is to think carefully about a situation or event and form an opinion about it, so that you can decide what to do.

Finally, 'stock-in-trade' refers to the typical characteristics or behaviour of someone or something while 'stock-still' means without moving, completely still.

From the above 'stalk' and 'stock' may sound the same but are very different in meaning. It is therefore important to be mindful of the differences. When in doubt consult a dictionary.

Dictionary Work

Check the meanings of the following words:

1. *stockholder*
2. *stockbroker*
3. *stock-control*
4. *stock market*
5. *substratum*
6. *umbrage*
7. *steeplechase*

41

Tends to Turn

'Tend' is sometimes confused with 'turn' when the intended meaning is 'incline' or 'move in a particular direction'. In the sentence, 'Your friends turn to laugh at you', the use of 'turn' is wrong. The correct word is 'tend'. So the sentence should read 'Your friends tend to laugh at you'.

Two reasons may account for this error. First, the meaning of 'tend', that is, 'move in a particular direction' probably misleads people to use the word 'turn' instead since 'turn' is basically used to signify movement or direction. The second reason may be the perceived closeness in pronunciation between the two words. 'Tend' is pronounced /tɛnd/ while 'turn' is pronounced /tɜ:n/. When the sound /d/ at the end of 'tend' is swallowed (that is, it is not articulated) it may sound like 'turn' especially if the speaker is not accustomed to making a distinction between /∊/ and /ɜ:/. We should remember that the vowel qualities are different: /ɜ:/ occurs in 'turn' /tɜ:n/. while /∊/ occurs in 'tend' /tɛnd/.

Now, let's explore other meanings of 'tend'. If something tends to happen, it happens often and so it is what usually happens. The meaning here is, to frequently behave in a particular way. For example: 'Ama tends to eat rice and stew for breakfast'.

People sometimes say 'I tend' when they want to appear modest about what they are saying or to reduce the force of a claim they are making. Example: 'I tend to think that's not a good solution'.

Another meaning of 'tend' is to look after something very carefully, especially in a loving way. For instance, you can say—'His mother tended him when he was very sick', or 'He looked forward to tending his sheep again'.

Furthermore, 'tend' may be used to mean work on a piece of land so that plant or crops will grow there; in other words, to cultivate the land. Example: 'They tend both the rice fields and the vegetable garden'.

Finally, if you tend to someone or something, you pay attention to them and deal with their problems and needs. Example sentences are: 'I have to tend to my students', and 'In his spare time he tends to the family business'.

This unit's heading 'Tends to Turn' captures the meanings of 'tend' and 'turn' in one phrase. It means inclined (tends) to move (turn).

Dictionary Work

Study the meanings of the following expressions:

1. *turn full circle*
2. *turn belly up*
3. *turn your nose up*
4. *turn a blind eye*
5. *turn over a new leaf*
6. *turn the knife in the wound*

42

Thick and Thin

The expression 'through thick and thin' means to continue to do something, however, bad the conditions or circumstances might be. For example, it may be used for a situation where one spouse continues to live with the other despite their bad circumstances (i.e., sudden poverty): 'She stayed with her husband through thick and thin'. As separate words 'thick' and 'thin' have certain idiomatic uses that are worth exploring.

Thick

A person who is thick with someone is very friendly with them. It is also used to show disapproval in informal English. Example: 'I didn't know you were thick with Kofi'. If you say that two people are 'as thick as thieves', you mean that they are very friendly indeed and don't seem to want other friends.

If things happen 'thick and fast', they happen very quickly and in large numbers. Example: 'Competition entries have been coming in thick and fast'.

'In the thick of' an activity or situation means you are very involved in it. Example: 'John is in the thick of his exams'. If someone's voice is thick, it is indistinct and sounds as if they are unable to speak clearly, for example because they have a cold or have drunk too much. Example: 'His voice sounded thick'.

If you say that someone is 'as thick as two short planks', you mean that they are very stupid indeed and do not seem to understand anything. This is also an informal expression.

Thin

We can also look at other expressions formed with 'thin'. If you describe people or businesses as having a 'thin time' it means they are not being very successful, often because economic conditions in general are not good. Example: 'The local papers are having a thin time'.

When you say that people or things are 'thin on the ground', you mean that there are not very many of them and so they are hard to find. Example: 'Good football players are still rather thin on the ground'.

When a joke or a story 'is wearing thin', it is begining to lose its effect because it has been repeated too many times Example: 'The joke had begun to wear very thin'. When your patience or your temper 'is wearing thin', you are begining to become impatient or angry. Example: 'Her patience will probably have worn thin by the end of the day'.

If an area 'thins out', it becomes less crowded because people are moving away. Example: 'Rural areas are thinning out as young people move to the cities'.

Dictionary Work

Study the meanings of the following words:

1. *fraternal*
2. *cretin*
3. *complicity*
4. *disperse*
5. *sparse*
6. *decimate*

43

Through and Thorough

The obvious homophone for "through" /Θru:/ is "threw" /Θru:/ (the past tense of "throw"), but the pair is not the focus of this unit Rather 'through' and 'thorough' /Θʌrə/, similar in spelling but divergent in pronunciation, provide an overriding motivation for discussion in the unit. In fact, they do share a common linguistic ancestry, 'through' having preceded 'thorough' in coming into the English language.

Through

Basically, 'through' means to move from one side or end of something (i.e., a space or hole) to the other. So you can go through a door, an area or a town. Examples: (1) Walk through that door to the Director's office (2) We drove through Tema. It may also be used in reference to a pervasive feeling, attitude, or quality. Example: 'Arrogance runs through the organisation'. This sentence means the attitude (i.e., arrogance) exists everywhere in the organisation.

Additionally, there are several idiomatic expressions formed with 'through'. A few are explained below. 'Drag somebody's name through the mire/mud' (to damage somebody's reputation by saying extremely insulting things about them.) 'Go through fire and water' (to experience many difficulties or dangers in order to achieve something). 'Hear something through the grapevine' (to hear news from someone who heard the news from someone else.) 'Go through the mill' (to receive or undergo the experiences or hardships needed to acquire a certain degree of skill or wisdom). 'Slip through somebody's fingers' (lose an opportunity or somebody through lack of care or effort). 'Thread your way through' (to move carefully through a crowded space, changing direction in order to avoid people or things).

Thorough

A thorough action or activity is one that is done very carefully and methodically so that nothing is overlooked. It is synonymous with 'exhaustive'. Example: 'The police did a thorough search of the building hoping to catch one of the armed robbers'. The adverb for thorough is 'thoroughly' while the noun is 'thoroughness'. The adjectival form is 'thorough', and it is used to refer to someone who is always very helpful and methodical in their work. Example: 'John is very thorough when marking his scripts'. 'Thorough' is also used to emphasize the great degree or extent of something. Example: 'I will give him a thorough reproof when he returns from the night club'. 'Thoroughly' meaning utterly or completely can be used in the following context: 'I thoroughly agree with the judge'.

We also have the words – 'thoroughbred', 'thoroughfare' and 'thoroughgoing'. 'Thoroughbred' refers to a horse that has parents that are of the same high quality breed. 'Thoroughfare' is a main road in a town or city which usually has the main shops along it and a lot of traffic. The expression 'No thoroughfare' is used on road signs to tell people not to use a road or path, for example because it is private property. It means 'No access'. A thoroughgoing action or quality is complete and full. Note that you can also spell this word with a hyphen. Example: 'He did a thorough-going study of the forest'.

Dictionary Work

Study the meanings of the following words and expressions:

1. *through and thorough*
2. *through a glass darkly*
3. *throughput*
4. *through traffic*
5. *unmitigated*
6. *meticulous*

44

Practice Exercise on Homophones

Below is a list of homophones. Look them up in a good dictionary, and take note of the following:

i. Pronunciation
ii. Meaning
iii. Part of speech
iv. Example phrases and sentences

air/heir/err
aural/oral
beach/beech
berth/birth/
bloc/block
boarder/border
born/borne
bridle/bridal
broach/brooch
cannon/canon
canvass/canvas
cast/caste
cereal/serial
cheap/cheep
click/clique
complement/compliment
cord/chord
core/corps
cue/queue
discreet/discrete
flair/flare
foreword/forward
fort/forte
gild/guild
gorilla/guerilla
grate/great
hangar/hanger
illicit/elicit
insight/incite
maybe/may be
peal/peel
plain/plane
pray/prey
sealing/ceiling
steal/steel
sweet/suite
toe/tow
vain/vane/vein
waive/wave
weather/whether

ENDNOTES

1 The phrase 'capacity building' used to mean manpower development has been popularised through its frequent use in the speeches of politicians and so-called development partners. 'Fast track' which means a route, course, or method which provides for more rapid results than usual came into vogue as a result of its use to describe courts whose proceedings had been computerised to accelerate the trial of people especially politicians who were said to have caused financial loss to the state. Used as a verb, 'fast track' means to accelerate the development or progress of a person or project.

'Zero tolerance' was one of the campaign slogans of the New Patriotic Party (NPP) in the 2000 parliamentary and presidential elections. It was used in the context 'zero tolerance for corruption'.

'Domestication' was the campaign slogan for the Ghana Consolidated People's Party (GCPP) led by Mr. Dan Lartey. Mr. Lartey personally popularised the word by using it, at the least opportunity, to punctuate his utterances. People tend to use it for humorous effects.

2 Refer to Ayto (1999) for further information on 'global village' (d. 1960). Note also 'global warming' (d. 1977).

3 See Levin (1995:78).

4 Readers who are interested in further exploring the meanings and connotations of 'tribe' and 'ethnicity' should consult both British-based and American-based corpora dictionaries.

5 See Merriam-Webster's (1989) for further explanation with examples of contexts in which 'money' and 'monies' have been used.

[6] 'Balanced' is listed in Dako (2003:34) as an example of a Ghanaianism and glossed as 'amount of money, change'.

[7] Dako (2003:60) provides an extensive explanation of the use of 'chop' in Ghana. Word combination forms she cites include: chop bar; chop fish; chop money; chop somebody/something small; chop time.

[8] Ayto (1999) puts the origin of the expression Catch-22 at 1961. According to him, the expression originates from a paradoxical rule postulated in the novel Catch-22 (1961, released as a film in 1970), by Joseph Heller, a US author. It means 'a supposed law or regulation containing provisions which are mutually frustrating; a set of circumstances in which one requirement, etc., is dependent upon another, which is in turn dependent upon the first.' Ayto documents contexts in which 'Catch-22' has been used.

[9] Dako (2003:203) glosses it as a word of excuse, also used as euphemism for excrement.

[10] Ayto (1999) says 'brain death' came into the English Language in 1964, 'brain-dead' in 1976 and 'brain drain' in 1963. According to Ayto 'brain death' was a concept introduced to define death more narrowly, in the face of medieval advances in keeping injured people alive artificially. He also explains that 'brain drain' was a journalistic coinage which achieved some success in the early 1960s, and continues to emerge from time to time when the phenomenon asserts itself. In Ghana, the expression came into vogue in the late 70s when many Ghanaian professionals left Ghana for Nigeria and other countries to seek better working conditions. See Ayto for exemplifications of contexts in which 'brain death', 'brain-dead' and 'brain drain' were used originally.

[11] Many grammar books deal with the issue of countable and uncountable nouns. For a comprehensive explanation see Quirk and Greenbaum (2000) [Pearson Education edition].

[12] It would be useful to read the explanations given in The Merriam Webster Dictionary; it is not only insightful but also lively.

[13] Dr. George Akaling-Pare, Department of Linguistics, University of Ghana in a personal communication.

[14] Pinker's (1995:402) preference for the distinction between 'disinterested' and 'uninterested' makes very interesting reading.

[15] *The Weekend Heritage,* 15th November 2002, Published by Heritage Communications, Accra. Kwabena Nyamekye was the pseudonym for the late Professor S. A. Nkrumah a former Director of the University of Ghana Business School.

[16] Another word that has the same pronunciation is 'rain' /rein/.

BIBLIOGRAPHY

American Heritage Dictionary. (1972, 1977). Boston: Houghton Mifflin.

Ayto, John. (1999). *20th Century Words.* Oxford: Oxford University Press.

Cambridge International Dictionary of English. (1995). Cambridge: Cambridge University Press.

Collins Cobuild English Dictionary. (1987). London and Glasgow: Collins.

Concise Oxford Dictionary. (1990). Oxford: Oxford University Press.

Dako, K. (2003). *Ghanaianisms: A Glossary.* Accra: Ghana Univeristies Press.

Flavell, Linda and Roger Flavell (2000) *Dictionary of Word* Origins. [Bookmart edition]. First published 1995. London: Kyle Cathie.

Levin, B. (1993). *English Verb Classes and Alternations.* Chicago: University of Chicago Press.

Longman Dictionary of Contemporary English (3rd Edition). (2000). Longman.

Marius, Richard. (1995). *A Writer's Companion.* (3rd Edition) New York: McGraw Hill.

McArthur, Tom. (Editor) (1992). *Oxford Companion to the English Language.* Oxford: Oxford University Press.

Merriam-Webster's Dictionary of English Usage. (1989). Springfield: Merriam-Webster's.

New Oxford Dictionary of English. (1998). Oxford: Oxford University Press.

Oxford Advanced Learner's Dictionary. (1989). 4th Edition, Oxford: Oxford University Press.

Oxford Advanced Learner's Dictionary. (2000) 6th Edition. Oxford: Oxford University Press. [Pearson Education Edition] Longman.

Pinker, S. (1994). *The Language Instinct.* Harper Perennial.

Questions of English. (1994). Oxford: Oxford University Press.

Quirk, Randolph and Sidney Greenbaum. (2000). *A University Grammar of English.*

Webster's Seventh New Collegiate Dictionary. (1967). Springfield: Merriam-Webster.

Webster's Ninth New Collegiate Dictionary. (1985). Springfield: Merriam-Webster.

Zimmer, B. (18 February 2011, accessed on 4 April 2011). Have your cake and eat it too. NYTimes.com

SUBJECT INDEX